T0062816

KASHMIR and Me

A True Tale of Surviving a Flood

RENU MITTAL

PARTRIDGE

Copyright © 2017 by Renu Mittal.

ISBN:	Hardcover	978-1-4828-8783-9
	Softcover	978-1-4828-8782-2
	eBook	978-1-4828-8781-5

All rights reserved. No part of this book may be used or reproduced by any means, graphic, electronic, or mechanical, including photocopying, recording, taping or by any information storage retrieval system without the written permission of the author except in the case of brief quotations embodied in critical articles and reviews.

Because of the dynamic nature of the Internet, any web addresses or links contained in this book may have changed since publication and may no longer be valid. The views expressed in this work are solely those of the author and do not necessarily reflect the views of the publisher, and the publisher hereby disclaims any responsibility for them.

Print information available on the last page.

To order additional copies of this book, contact
Partridge India
000 800 10062 62
orders.india@partridgepublishing.com

www.partridgepublishing.com/india

In The Loving Memory Of My Beloved Husband
Anil Mittal

(13.11.1962 to 20.3.2001)

My only sermon to my dearest sons

Kashish and Parth
Nothing in the world means more to me than you two.

Despite all dilemma
Let your enthu never waver, be not crooked but right,
Though time will test thy toils, have heart and hold your
target tight.

World may betray
Never give in vim, let not fire in your belly quiet,
gather all your guts, march forward be it day, be it night.

See.. the sky is a heartbeat away
with all might demand Dhananjay to grace sight,
dare once last, decree of fate will turn gait and thine fortune
ignite.

Though thy show be slow,
You will be the one not bow but attain rainbow!

Disclaimer

In my book '**Kashmir and Me**' though I have tried to recreate a true portrait of all the incidents, events, locales and conversations from my memories of them still I have made some changes in the names of individuals, places and events just to meet the requisites of the storyline and to maintain their anonymity in some instances. I may have altered or elaborated some characteristics and identifying details such as physical properties of Ch2 Hotel and the role played by Local Kashmiris, JK police and our Indian Army *Jawans in evacuating and rescuing the entrapped crowd but nowhere I intend to question the reverent image of any of the concerned authorities or individuals. Although I have made every effort to ensure that the information in this book is correct, I do not assume any liability to anybody for any disruption caused by errors or omissions resulting from negligence or any other cause. I may not be held liable, or responsible, for anything based on what I wrote.

ABOUT THE AUTHOR

Renu Mittal, born on 6th November 1965 in New Delhi, India to Mr. & Mrs. KR Aggarwal, is the youngest of five siblings.

After completing her Master's Degree in commerce she married Mr Anil Mittal in 1987. He was a successful businessman and a devotional singer of Lord Krishna.

Her married life was blissful and they were blessed with two sons Kashish and Parth. Life was smooth till she had to face the sudden demise of her beloved husband in 2001, after spending splendid 14 years of married life.

Now leading life with two small kids without any financial aid, proved to be too hostile. She had to encounter tough times and battle humiliation and pennilessness to earn her livelihood. She faced a single mother's desperation every second to nurture her kids in the best plausible way, sustaining her own identity as well.

Her determination, persistent efforts and the grace of Almighty made her conquer her fears and chart her own course in life.

She witnessed all gay and grey shades of life but came through with flying colours. Being an ardent theist, she attributes her entire success to the Almighty.

At present she runs "Renu Mittal Concepts" Academy and imparts education with her kids.

PREFACE

This book is a true account of my two visits to Kashmir: the first in 1998 with my husband Anil and my two sons, Kashish and Parth, and the second with a group of nine people in 2014, when the valley experienced the worst flooding in more than a century.

During the first visit, I saw a valley too elegant and magnificent to be described. But due to political turmoil, every inch was a picture of utter gloom. Even so we were full of guts and gaiety as our family of four was together. We saw more Border Security Force personnel than the locals, still we felt secure under Anil's protective shield.

In September 2014, I set out for Kashmir again with my two nieces and their families to witness the marvellousness of Kashmir. But most unexpectedly we were caught in the massive flood which devastated the valley that month.

It is a real story of indefatigable efforts of our group against all odds, of rising and falling hopes and of exhibiting unfathomable capacity to tide over all challenges and extreme distress to survive.

Our children showcased extreme bravery and the farsightedness and meticulous approach of the captain of our troupe, Mr. Sanjay Mittal, saved us from the jaws of death.

I hope this story will inspire people not to panic in times of distress but keep calm and face critical times with a brave front.

I dedicate all my accomplishments to Lord Krishna who did not abandon me during perilous times on the journey of my life.

May He shower His blessings on all.

Jai Shri Shyam

7th September 2014

Around 2:30 a.m.

The hotel was thundering with panic. "The bridge has broken! The bridge has broken!"

"Vacate the room! Run to the second floor! Hurry up!"

The cries were spreading like wildfire. Water had entered the hotel building. People were running helter-skelter as if the place had been struck by a violent storm.

When I looked out of the window of my room, I couldn't believe my eyes. There was a sea of water all around! My mind froze. I blinked a few times wondering if the water was for real or I was only dreaming.

But the chaos outside the room assured me I wasn't hallucinating. We were indeed caught in the vicious jaws of an enormous water giant that was ready to swallow us any moment.

Try to see the scene through my eyes who was witnessing it personally.

The night had begun like an unpleasant dream. As soon as I started to doze off, I had to get up as waiters, staff members and guests were making a lot of noise on our floor. I tried hard to block it out and go to sleep but couldn't manage to get even a wink. Whenever I tried to close my eyes, the din in the corridor seemed to grow louder. Beyond annoyed, I stepped out of my room in a rage.

This is what I saw––

A group of men were deeply engrossed in a serious but loud conversation. It looked very ominous. I, at once, retreated into my room and bolted the door shut.

It was around 1:30 a.m.

I peeped out of the window of my room that overlooked a courtyard and was aghast on seeing many people clad in white **kurta pyjamas[1]* talking vociferously. Their menacing tone made my skin crawl.

I was gripped with a sudden fear. I doubted whether all those tales of riots that we had been hearing since partition were going to come true. The men outside were perhaps a gang of anarchists preparing for some sort of attack on us or it might be worse than that.

---

*   *For all Italic words refer glossary at page no. 343*
[1]   *loose collarless long shirt and lose pants*

The human heart is weak. Whenever it finds things not going as expected, or sees anything even a little unusual, it loses control and starts weaving all manner of stories, adding fuel to the confusion and fear. Our hearts, though timid, are tamed with great difficulty.

I was unable to take the chaos in my stride and immediately called at the reception to ask what was going on.

They told me that people living close to the hotel had come in to take shelter due to flooding in their localities. But they assured me there was nothing to worry about. Guests at the hotel were absolutely safe.

We can call it fate that a Muslim person, even if he belongs to a very principled and religious family, hasn't been able to win complete faith of other communities around the world. People generally see him suspiciously. He is often a target of distrust, even though a major portion of the Muslim population is not involved in any violent activities. Muslims are generally very simple and adhere to their religious teachings. And most of the community dislikes people among them who jeopardize others lives.

The idiom, 'One dirty fish spoils the whole pond' stands true in this context. Due to the deeds of a handful of miscreants––of any nation, state, community, sex, or religion around the world––people of other communities have to suffer. Their own group suffers because others become suspicious of the whole lot.

Why did I doubt the motives of a crowd that had never caused me any harm? On the contrary, all Muslims and Kashmiris we had come across during our trip had been extremely hospitable and had tried to serve us the best way they could.

So why did I get so scared on seeing a group of people just because they were wearing a certain kind of attire?

Where and when did this mistrust begin? Where is that era when people from all religions were an inseparable part of one Hindustan and lived in harmony? Who ignited the spark of this division? Had it been the Mughal emperors, the British or our politicians? Or is it our own prejudice that has led us down this path of fear?

I was not an exception to this form of prejudice.

The commotion outside my room, instead of settling, was only growing louder. I just couldn't get back to sleep. Neither did my fear subside despite all the rationalizing. I called at the reception again after ten minutes. Almost angrily I said, "Is everything all right? Why are these people not lowering their voices? Why don't you ask them to move to some other place? Why don't you do something to ensure your guests are not disturbed?"

The receptionist replied, "Ma'am, I am very sorry for the inconvenience, and I will do the needful. But please calm down. Let me assure you there is nothing to worry at all."

The man tried his best to convince me that I wasn't in any danger. But I don't know why I had suddenly become so suspicious that I didn't believe him. The glimpse of locals outside my room had set my mind jumping in all directions. I just couldn't shake off the feeling that something was amiss and I was not safe.

Since the day we had landed in Kashmir, we had come across a very gentle, soft-spoken population who respected and welcomed its guests. They all wore the same white *kurta pyjamas*[2] that the men outside were wearing. Then why had seeing similar people tonight turned me into a bundle of nerves?

I tried to calm down, but failed.

I stood near the window thinking what to do next. I was both scared and annoyed at having being disturbed. I took a deep breath, slunk into the bed and made another attempt to catch some sleep.

But relaxing had become impossible. I tried to wake up Parth but he was sleeping so soundly, I gave up. When the tumult outside swelled, I became so scared I forcefully woke him up and rattled off what was going on.

Instead of being concerned, he snapped at me, "Mumma, why are you up at this hour? Who told you to choose CH2 hotel? These are local hotels and you shouldn't expect peace

---

[2]   *loose collarless long shirt and lose pants*

5

here. Now, please close your eyes, be quiet, and let me sleep at least."

He took the entire matter casually and went back to sleeping like a log.

I, on the other hand, lay fully awake.

Suddenly a roar went up, "Run! The bridge has broken. Hurry up!"

I jumped to the window and craned my neck to see as far as I could. The earth was snatched away under my feet! A huge wave of water was rolling towards the hotel. I started shaking.

Only an hour back I had complained to the receptionist against the disturbance. That reception area, visible from my window, was completely flooded! It was a single-storied covered area in the middle of two blocks of the hotel. It could be seen from the large, sealed windows of many rooms including ours.

Peering through the thick glass, I wondered from where so much water had burst into the compound? Within less than an hour, our hotel had become an island floating in the middle of a sea! But how did so much water appear on land so soon?

"No, this can't be real," my head screamed. "I'm sure I'm either dreaming or fatigue and sleep deprivation are finally getting to me."

I shook Parth again and this time he got up at once and asked, "What's going on Mumma? Why is there so much noise?"

No words came out of my mouth. I just pointed to the window and slumped in the chair.

He ran to see through it and shouted, "Oh, my God! How did so much water get in here? Mumma! Let's get out of this place!"

It didn't take him even a second to realize that our hotel was trapped in the middle of a flash flood. If we didn't hurry, we would drown within minutes.

Out of the blue, we were staring at death.

We glanced at each other with blank eyes. That look was so strange that I will never forget it. There was no sorrow, pain, love or any other feeling. Neither of us knew what to say or how to console the other. In that moment, there was only shock and no time to show concern for anyone.

We had not even steadied our breaths when Anshu banged on our door in panic. He asked us to move upstairs immediately.

We tried to gather our things that were scattered in all corners of the room, but realizing the urgency, we only took bags and suitcases that were within reach and ran as fast as we could to the floor above.

In the hasty dash out of the room, we forgot to collect any eatables from the fridge, Parth's shoes, trousers, my night suit, slippers and toiletries from the bathroom.

All three of us rushed to the second floor into room no. 2012, where Anju was staying. Her kids, Anshu and Radhika, were in room no. 2013. Manoj, Neha and Aarav had already arrived in 2012. I don't know how they reached there so fast but they were there before us. The room was packed to capacity with all nine members of our group assembled there with the luggage. Everyone stood around bewildered, trying to process what was happening.

Nobody said anything except Aarav. He began crying for his toy that had been left behind in his room. Soon he made his way to Shakku, a kid he had befriended at the hotel. Shakku and his parents had been staying in room no. 1014. They had also reached the second floor and were in the next room. Both Shakku had Aarav began crying over one thing or the other that was left behind in their rooms on the lower floors. All efforts to pacify them were unsuccessful.

Finally, Parth scolded them, "Either you keep quiet, or I will throw you in this water." He lifted Aarav and showed him the water level through the window.

His trick worked. Both boys kept quiet for some time and stopped complaining about their missing belongings. The episode diverted everyone's mind and we relaxed for a few moments.

But nobody knew what to do.

There was a recliner seat in the room and Radhika had been sitting on it for a while. Having nothing else to do, the older kids started horsing around with the chair and soon an argument broke out over who will sit on it next.

The recliner was the only distraction in the cramped room.

Outside the room fear reigned and we strictly prohibited our kids from stepping out. Anything could happen. Guests, staff members and other people were rushing about shocked at the sudden appearance of the deluge in CH2.

Aarav refused to let the teenagers enjoy. He threatened, "This is my chair. I will sit on it. If you don't let me, I will start crying again."

The older boys scolded him but Aarav wasn't about to be cowed down or give up. The boys folded their hands and begged, "For God's sake, Aarav, just be quiet."

He only screamed louder. Anshu lost it then. He got up from his chair and gave Aarav a slap. He yelled, "Now sit on the damn chair and don't talk to us, or I'll slap you again."

These little skirmishes kept our minds off the danger and helped the kids get through the wait.

Suddenly, there was a loud commotion outside and it caught everyone's attention. We heard that a waiter was still stuck on the ground floor and other staff members were trying to pull him up through the broken staircase. His shirt was stuck in a nail. He was hurt and was bleeding badly. However, after some maneuvering by the staff, he was pulled up to safety.

The incident made the kids realize that the situation was more serious than they thought. They restrained their wits and all jokes and arguments ceased. Nobody demanded anything and they went back quietly to their respective places by the window and watched the water level rise.

No one could have imagined then, the terrifying trauma that was to follow.

At 4:00 a.m.

We were stuck in one room, watching through the window the alarming surge of water. Everyone including people from nearby localities were all equally tense.

I was looking intently through the window pane at a ladder that was leaning on the hotel block across ours. That block was the taller wing of the hotel connected via the single storied reception area. Water had been steadily swallowing its steps one after another. In only half an hour, almost five of its sections disappeared.

We couldn't take our eyes off the water as it went up inch-by-inch right before our eyes.

Soon, the ladder and the flowerpots, along with the doors, chairs, and the big table in the courtyard disappeared under water. The first floor of our hotel and room no. 1012, in which I had been staying with my younger son Parth, was also half gone.

Just imagine if we had still been sleeping in that room! We too would have drowned. In just over an hour, we had watched things go from absolutely normal to completely life-threatening.

Though we had a narrow escape from death, the knowledge of what could have happened chilled our bones. I took a deep breath, pulled out a bottle from the refrigerator, and gulped large mouthfuls of water in one go. Still I was panting, so Parth made me lie down on the bed.

But when I closed my eyes, I could only see images of us sleeping in 1012. No one woke us up and we found ourselves in water. We were trying our best to stay above the water level, but despite our efforts we were gradually drowning and were about to be devoured by the flood.

I screamed out loud.

On opening my eyes, I found Parth beside me and we were all right. Parth shook me, and to divert my mind he asked, "Mumma, where are the suitcase keys?"

I stumbled out of the delirium and replied that they were in my handbag.

But I couldn't avoid the thought that if we hadn't rushed to the second floor, we would not be alive.

We must have done some good karma in our past lives and that had helped us survive such a catastrophic tragedy.

So I thought in that moment.

The omens of what was in store didn't stop. The water was almost 3ft of our room on the first floor. It was rising at such alarming speed that we realized it would burst into the second floor soon. If we did not make arrangements to shift immediately, we would be in grave danger.

Those were tormenting moments for us. No one in the room had any idea what to do, where to go, how to go and whether any other place around us was safer than where we were?

This was the scene at hotel CH2 on Broadway Road, Srinagar, on 7th September 2014.

Our group comprised of nine members:

Renu and Parth Mittal––myself and my 19-year-old younger son.
Anju and Sanjay Mittal––my niece and her husband.
Deepanshu (Anshu) and Radhika (Radhu) Mittal––Anju's 20-year-old son and 15-year-old daughter.
Neha (Golu) and Manoj Gupta––another niece and her husband
Aarav (Aaru) Gupta––Neha's 4-year-old son.

Our group had reached Kashmir on 2nd September 2014, and since that day it had been raining non-stop. But nobody had imagined that the rain would turn into such a colossal flood.

We had come to stay in the hotel after spending two lavish days in Gulmarg at Hotel Khyber, but had unfortunately got stranded in the unexpected flood. Many guests like us in the hotel were facing the same fate.

As we sat in room 2012 coming to terms with the precarious situation we were in, Sanjay came and announced that the best thing would be for all stranded people to shift to the opposite block, the taller wing of CH2.

The two blocks were about a hundred feet apart. One had three floors and the other had five. The reception area on the ground floor with a sloping roof connected the two wings. This area was totally submerged, with only the top of its roof peaking over water.

The only choice left was to shift to the taller wing. It was speculated that this could provide us a better survival option. Else, we were all doomed for sure.

Sanjay said, "Leave all luggage in the room and only carry your bag packs with eatables, cash and a few other useful things that we might need." He stressed repeatedly we keep the bags light and not get greedy about carrying all our expensive stuff.

He reasoned, "We can get all things dear to us anytime in Delhi but if and only if we are able to keep ourselves alive.

So don't waste time in stressing about what to take. And hurry up!"

Everyone backed his proposal. Parth, Anshu and Neha at once began stuffing available food from the fridge in their bag packs along with digi-cams, mobiles, cash and a few other expensive items.

When this announcement was being made, I was in the rest room brushing my teeth and a tiny toothpaste tube was in my hand.

In my nervousness, I slid the tube in my jacket's pocket. I never imagined then how that small tube would prove to be of tremendous use later on.

I went out, took some chocolates from Parth's bag and gave one to each member to keep in it their pockets just in case we ran out of food before the water receded.

Everyone got busy preparing for the shift to the other block.

We were facing an unknown journey. No one had any clue what was about to happen. All had to surrender to the will of the Lord willingly or unwillingly as nothing was in their control.

To foresee that we would survive was no guarantee. But we were hoping against hope that we would.

Sanjay took the lead and spoke to the staff about planning the evacuation. He appealed to every staff member and tried to convince them of the urgent need to leave the building at once. Else, all would drown considering the speed at which water was rising.

Sanjay maintains his cool in every situation, focusing only on what needs to be done. He formed a team of 20 volunteers who also agreed unanimously that shifting to the other building was the only option.

Though that building was not very far away from the one we were in, the distance between the two had been converted into a deep pool of water and its level was rapidly increasing. The reception area and all things between the two blocks were submerged under water.

Till then everyone had been praying for deliverance from the calamity. But as soon as it became clear that shifting to the other building was the only way to save ourselves, we were gripped with fear wondering how we would cross to the other side.

But we had no choice and our options couldn't have been clearer. Either stay in the same building worrying about the depth of water and most certainly die, or make efforts to reach the other end and perhaps survive.

The situation demanded 'sink or swim'.

But what if someone fell into the water while crossing? The chances of their survival were almost nil.

I don't know what the team discussed for so long, but five-six boys went around all rooms announcing that the shift would happen along a railing that ran around the two buildings but was close enough to both on the southern end. They, in fact, showed us the railing from our window. Only the upper part of the iron railing was visible as the 10-inch thick wall it was fixed on was almost completely under water.

Even the thought that we had to step on that narrow invisible wall and slide along it holding the railing for support sent shivers down our spines.

Almost everyone rebelled against the idea. But the boys encouraged us saying, "Ma'am, of course it looks dangerous but if you are careful and cautious, you will easily walk across the wall holding the railing."

Those boys were around 20-25 years of age. A few were strongly built but most looked skinny. I have to admit they had a lot of courage. They were able to convince us all to give the wall a try.

One of them, with dark red hair, was talking to people very kindly without any trace of fear or unease. In fact, all of them were very pleasant and hardly seemed perturbed by the situation. We wondered how they kept their cool, and were embarrassed at how scared we were compared to them.

Ujjwal, who was staying in the room no. 1015 and was travelling with his wife and little daughter, couldn't resist asking the redheaded young man, "How are you so calm?

It's wonderful how patiently you are dealing with this panic-stricken crowd."

The boy replied, "*Bhaijaan*[3], there is nothing new in this. We Kashmiris are used to facing uncertainties and calamities that appear out of nowhere. Only the faces of the emergencies differ. We have become used to coping with this or that."

While his words revealed the tragedy of Kashmir, strangely, his demeanor gave us strength to try our luck with the crossing.

The local Kashmiris, who had come to take shelter in CH2 from the neighbouring localities, were taking the lead in figuring out ways to move from this place. Otherwise, most of the guests like us were sitting scared bemoaning our luck. Only a few among us like Sanjay, Ujjwal and Mr. Mehra were focusing on what was to be done. With every tick of the clock, all understood that it would be better to flow with the flow rather than pondering what would happen if we did this or that.

Sometime after the boys had informed everyone, we were told we would have to leave the room but without any luggage. It would be impossible to carry suitcases on our shoulders across the wall. Life was more important than stuff.

All we had to focus on was survival.

Anshu, Parth and Manoj placed all suitcases one on top of the other on the highest shelf of an almirah. They decided

---

[3]   *brother*

to take only three bag packs, which Parth, Anshu and Neha would carry.

On parting with my luggage, I was hit with remorse. My things––the dresses, shoes, cosmetics, spectacles, the newly bought shawls and stoles and all other stuff which had been so dear to me only a couple of hours ago now stood nowhere in the list of priorities.

How could we leave those beloved articles without giving a second thought to them?

I was filled with repentance. I felt as if my brown suitcase was screaming aloud and asking, "Is this your love? I have always been with you in times of happy vacations and now you are abandoning me without even gracing me with a concerned look."

Though I was feeling somewhat guilty, I was helpless.

In the corridor outside, staff members were asking everyone to be on alert as evacuation was about to begin. Our turn could come any moment.

Tension mounted with every passing minute and I had to get my emotions under control as many challenges awaited outside. We sensed only a few minutes of normal breaths were guaranteed. There was no certainty we would be able to accomplish the task of holding onto the railing and maintaining a foothold on the narrow wall as we crossed. If anyone failed to or dropped into water, they would certainly meet their end.

Parth was trying to pep me up by saying, "Mumma, you are a supermom! You will come first in this race, I can bet! Nothing can make you go weak. You are always full of energy and you are my inspiration. You can't give up. I'm here with you. Don't worry! Come on now, take on the adventure with your usual gusto."

He asked, "If you want to carry something more from your suitcase, I will stuff it in my bag without letting anybody know. Should I take your 27K shawl you purchased yesterday? You just tell me what you want."

I blessed my dear son in my heart. "How much I love you! You are so concerned about your mother's likes and dislikes even in these grave moments."

His words made me feel so wanted and loved that I got up energetically. I vowed I wouldn't give up and try my best to survive this calamity. Both my children still needed me and I was willing to go to any extent to live for them.

As the final time of leaving our room approached, we all shivered within our bodies but nobody showed their fear. The same was true of the entire crowd. Everyone knew that the wall was the only hope so they had to take the chance without a word.

We all wished to make a last call to our families in Delhi and listen to their voices because after that moment, our fate was foggy.

But the network was poor and available only on Sanjay's mobile. He asked everyone to exchange only a few words with their family members. We started calling our 'person' as fast as we could.

Overcome with emotion, all burst into tears. We were unable to communicate clearly with our loved ones.

When my turn came, I called my elder son Kashish who hadn't come with us and was in Delhi at that time. In a broken voice I uttered, "Kasha, I love you a lot. We are stranded in hotel CH2 at Broadway Road behind Jhelum river in almost 13-14 feet of water. This may be our last call and I won't be able to contact you further for some time. So be brave and take care of yourself."

I could sense his trembling voice. He was only able to utter, "Mumma! Mumma!" It seemed as if his voice froze, and he was unable to speak. I understood that my dear son was terrified out of his wits but I didn't have any time to console him. We both wished to say more to each other but the call got disconnected.

All the ink and paper in the world will fall short to explain how I felt in that moment. It seemed as if a huge chunk of my heart was mercilessly ripped off and left to bleed.

All I could think was, "Oh, Kashish! If you were also here with me, I wouldn't have any regrets." Not that I wanted him to suffer with me. It was the thought of him all alone back home that broke my heart. I just wanted the solace of being together.

I prayed, "God, if somehow you can send my Parth to Delhi so that the two brothers can be together to brave the upheavals of life, I will accept my death without regrets."

Teary eyed, I stood still for a few moments gazing out of the window.

Parth suddenly asked me if I had taken out all the money from the suitcase and if there was any other valuable article I wished to carry. I shifted my focus to his words and came back to the present moment and told him that I had.

The time had come to risk our lives to save it.

It was 6 a.m.

The team of volunteers made a strategy about how to go to the other block.

Two staff members and three local boys would go back to the first floor. The danger was that though the water was only up to the waist level, it could go up at any moment.

Their plan was to smash the window pane of room no. 1012 where Parth and I had been staying. They would use broken logs or whatever was available to break the 5-by-5 thick glass. But it wasn't going to be easy.

It wasn't easy to walk through a room filled with 3ft of water, but the boys were determined. They had no idea what lay beneath the water and what they might step on or bump into. They held each other's hands firmly, and moved one cautious step at a time. It was like making way through a dense jungle where nothing is visible ahead. One boy's foot got stuck between the legs of a broken stool. He fell and was injured but he didn't give up. The other boys came forward to lend him a helping hand and all again continued with the plan.

The group slowly succeeded in making their way to the window and breaking it, thus igniting a ray of hope in the nervous crowd.

While the boys were risking their lives to make way for the next step of evacuation, I wandered off to the terrace to take some snaps of the devastated vicinity. While climbing the staircase, I saw staff members running around and picking food items from wherever they could. They had collected many Maggie packets, sugar sachets, jam bottles, soft drink tins, bread, butter, salt, oil canisters etc. from the kitchen and other rooms. They were carrying all these items to the top floor. I climbed the staircase after them and saw them placing all items in a small room on the terrace and covering them with many layers of plastic sheets. I really admired their sincere attempts.

I glanced around from the terrace and was dumbstruck! Nothing but water all around. The second floors of houses around were already under water. Many cars, chairs, tables, utensils, wooden pieces, and even cattle were either drowning or floating around. Animals were trying to save themselves but despite desperate efforts, they were losing the battle. Their painful moans could be heard on the terrace. Though heartbroken at their condition, people tried to ignore the dance of death before their eyes and fixed their gaze on other chores. A dog and a cow somehow reached the roof of a tall house and lay there dead with exhaustion.

The locals were standing on the terraces of their homes, distress writ large on their faces. Some were trying to salvage whatever they could from their inundated homes.

Instead of doing something useful, I started taking pictures like a maniac. I felt a sudden urge to capture all I could of the devastated area.

All of a sudden I heard a scream "Help! Help!" A male voice shouted from somewhere nearby.

I scoured the watery expanse to see where it had come from. My eyes found a man who was half under water and was screaming for help. He was flailing his hands and legs wildly and trying to keep his head above water.

But the strength in his body was no match to the force of the current. People who seemed to be his family were clamouring to save him and crying and screaming.

A few boys ripped off a door and threw it to him so he could get a hold of it and float. Someone threw a rope towards him and asked him to grab one end of it.

I spotted a policeman standing silently near a wall watching the drowning man. I begged him, "Sir, please do something to help that man. He is about to drown."

He replied, "Madam, if you think you can do something for him, you are most welcome. I can't save him."

I could not process the indifferent attitude of that policeman. I turned my face away from the sight of the drowning man. Panic gripped me completely in that moment and I started sobbing.

His screams compelled me to turn towards him again.

Terror had paralyzed the man and he was not able to grab either the door or the rope. Very quickly the vast expanse of water ran over him making his shrieks inaudible to the crowd. Within a few minutes only, water had swallowed a living man right before my eyes. The crowd on the roofs stood still like lifeless objects.

It hit me then just how much danger we were in. If anyone fell into the water, they were not going to survive.

All I could hear were screams of dying animals and desperate people shouting without any clear thing to say or convey. Surrounded by such trauma, why was I so keen on taking snaps?

The novel 'The Diary of a Young Girl' by Anne Frank had always been a book close to my heart. Anne, a Jewish girl, and seven other members of her family were forced to hide themselves in a secret annex for almost two years during World War II. They were hiding from Hitler and his Nazis.

In hiding, she wrote a diary in which she provided a lens on Jewish life in Hitler-occupied Amsterdam. She learnt quickly how to abandon the trappings of her privileged childhood and adjust to the critical times. Anne was just 13-years-old and she poured herself into the diary as she saw death getting closer every day for almost two years. Later, the whole family was sent to concentration camps and died of starvation. Her father, Mr. Otto Frank, was the sole survivor who published her diary after her death.

Like Anne, we were also nearing death. Like her, I felt compelled to record my ordeal. I felt the need to share the spectacle of a drowning Kashmir with anyone who would find my camera.

After clicking from every angle, I came down sobbing.

When Sanjay saw me with the digi-cam in my hand, he lost it. "What is wrong with you? You want to risk your life to click a few photographs? Do you understand just how much trouble we are in?" I didn't say anything and lost myself in the crowd to avoid more rebuke.

I couldn't get the shrieks of the drowning man out of my head. I had witnessed a horrifying tragedy and I was completely shaken. I wanted to tell everyone what I had seen but nobody had time for others' tales. They were all grappling alone, trying to come to terms with the horror of the situation.

Our room was slowly receding into silence as our turn to cross approached.

Outside the room, the locals were making arrangements to shift the entire crowd to the other wing. It was not an easy task to make so many people step one by one on that narrow wall to the other side. Especially a crowd that was so petrified.

This was going to be the shifting process––

We were to go down to the first floor, which was 3.5 feet in water, and then make our way to the smashed window from where we had to exit.

The rescue team was divided into groups.

The first group was a team of six Kashmiri Muslims, who would try the passage first, and if all went well, the rest of the stranded crowd would follow.

The second team comprised of guests––tourists like Sanjay, Mr. Mehra, Monu, Ujjwal, and six more volunteers. Their main task was to keep people lined up outside room no. 1012 so that everyone could go through that window in an orderly manner. It was not an easy task at all. Almost 200 people were stranded in the hotel. And they were becoming increasingly restless. No one wanted to wait or be the last one to leave. Pushing and shoving began. Little scuffles broke out. No one knew for sure what to do, but many were more than willing to air their opinions about how things should proceed.

The duty of the third group, which was mainly the staff members and two bouncers, was to maintain peace and send five people at a time to enter the room. They were standing right at the door so that no one went in out of turn.

Three sturdy men, all locals, stood inside the room to help people wade through the water, reach the window and climb through it to the other side and step onto the wall. Though they were all very attentive in trying to ensure people didn't cut themselves on broken glass, they had to push people out as time was short and the crowd was huge.

Once people went out of the window, they were on their own. They had to step onto the 10-inch wall, whose left side was under water. They would hold the railing on the right side and cross over to the other building.

They would reach a section of the reception area roof that was still above water. From there, they would have to climb into the other block through another smashed window.

The roof of the reception area was not a proper, cemented roof at all. It was made of some flimsy material and didn't look too strong. It took a great deal of courage to risk stepping on it. Since it was the only way to save their skins, everybody was willing to brave it.

The first team took the lead to reach the roof one by one, and by the grace of God, they crossed without any incident. A collective sigh of relief was heard at this success. After all, the lives of so many people were dependent on that first attempt and the situation could have turned fatal at any time.

All this while we had been chanting God's name sitting in room no. 2012. We hadn't joined the queue yet, but Anshu and Parth kept us updated about what was going on. We were anxious yet motionless at the same time. No one knew what would happen. The thought of risking our lives to save it was overwhelming.

Manoj had been given the responsibility of taking care of all of us in the room and not let anybody go out unnecessarily, especially his son Aarav. When the situation stabilized a bit, we would join the queue.

The process of shifting began. The crowd copied the first groups' manner of walking across. We were watching them from our window above and for every person on the wall we would cross our fingers.

I also saw a kitten struggling hard to save its life. She decided the way to do it was copy people and walk the wall. The beautiful mass of the cat's body had shrunk to a ball of fur due to freezing water and fear. When I saw it reaching the roof alive, I was strangely happy after having seen so many cows, dogs and even birds drowning.

Soon, one person at a time, the mass of people in our building began to melt. Our turn was nearing and we had almost gathered courage to cross the wall when suddenly a man in his late sixties lost balance and fell into the water. All our courage vanished. It looked like he would certainly drown. His family members began shouting for somebody to help him. Luckily, the man grabbed the edge of the roof and hung on to it.

We had seen similar scenes in movies many times but had never felt the terror we felt then.

Two men from the other end rushed to rescue him. Even though they succeeded in holding his hand, it wasn't easy to pull him up as he was heavy. Every time they got him up half way, their grip on him would loosen. In their third attempt, they were finally able to pull him up all the way.

After this scare the process resumed.

It was two little boys' turn to cross. But just having witnessed the accident, they froze. People tried to encourage them gently but they stood still, not moving an inch. The crowd was getting fidgety and the rising water level wasn't helping. They had to be moved somehow. Finally, their father threatened them with dire consequences and managed to send them across.

The queue started moving again and our turn came closer. When it arrived, we started shivering, but there was no way out. We had to journey across that deadly chasm if we wanted to be safe.

When we reached the entrance of the room, two men, also from Delhi, tried to get in saying that they were part of our group. The bouncers stopped them and a scuffle ensued. In the melee, I scrapped my ankle and it started bleeding. But there was no time to pay it any attention and I kept moving through the waist high water.

The room was unrecognizable from a few hours ago! Chairs, mugs, clothes, towels and many other things were floating around. People who entered the room had to step very cautiously as they couldn't see what they might step on.

Radhu was the first in our group to reach the window. When her turn came, she suddenly went back to her mother saying, "I won't go first."

So Anshu, who was next in line, started slowly but reached the roof on the opposite side safely. Then Anju pushed Radhu to go, advising, "Don't look down at the water. Just go straight like Anshu did."

Radhu, trembling and stumbling a bit, crossed too. Anju followed her. The problem was Aaru. He began to cry, bawling, "I'll not go Papa! I'll fall in water! Save me Papa! Save me!"

People who were behind us in the line got irritated and some even said, "You people go back to the end of the line if your son is not ready. Let others go."

But we couldn't let the chance go by, so Sanjay told Neha, "You go. We'll bring him." Neha went ahead. Parth shouted at Aaru, "If you don't go, we'll push you and you might fall into the water then. See that bouncer? I'm calling him and he'll push. But if you move quietly like the others, you'll get your bag of chips and chocolates, which your Mumma has taken. Otherwise, we will eat all of those things and you won't get any."

This threatening and cajoling had no impact whatsoever. Aaru wasn't ready and kept crying. A bouncer sternly said, "Sir, you leave him all alone in this wing. All of you go."

That threat of being left all alone scared Aaru suitably and he agreed to go with Manoj. "Hold the railing tight and move slowly. Papa is with you," we guided him.

It was my turn next, but I asked Parth to go before me.

He flatly refused, "I'll go only after you. So Mumma don't waste time arguing. *Jijaji*[4] and I will have no problems crossing."

I had to agree and stepped forward. On the first step itself I felt I won't be able to make it and looked back. When I saw a large body of anxious people waiting for their turns, I mustered courage and took the second step. My ankle was still bleeding and I was hobbling.

My grip on the railing was so firm that my knuckles turned white. Even so, every moment it seemed as if the railing would give way and fall with me in the water. I didn't look down as I had been strictly advised against it. But while moving, my wandering eyes couldn't control themselves and fell on the water and on the 10-inch wall I was walking on. My heart sank and courage took to its heels. Instead of moving further, my feet froze half way to the other side. I could hear Parth shouting, "Move Mumma! Move! You're about to reach!"

---

[4] *brother-in-law (sister's husband)*

But my head and legs were not ready to coordinate with each other. The destination was only a few feet away but my feet refused to budge. I could neither go back nor go forward. I found myself between the devil and the deep blue sea. For a few minutes, my whole body stood motionless. But Parth's shouts and others' encouragement and anger compelled my legs to defrost and I inched ahead till I reached the other side.

Soon after me, Parth and Sanjay too reached the roof.

Drudgery drains all veins,
But pays handsome gains.

Thank God, nothing went wrong. Bit by bit everyone hit the target and from the smaller wing of CH2 reached the other side safely. Somehow the thought of crossing had proved more terrifying than the actual task itself. I again thanked the Lord that nothing went wrong and the whole group managed to cross.

The last team of six people was standing at the other end to help new comers. They had made a little space to stand on the roof.

When I saw these people, I was taken aback. This was the same group of locals in white *kurta pyjamas*[5] whose sight had frightened me a few hours ago when I had seen them shouting and growling in the reception area. At that time,

---

[5] *loose collarless long shirt and lose pants*

they had looked like a gang of goons whose muscular bodies and attire had petrified me.

But the same group turned out to be *masiha*[6], the saviours, who were risking their lives to save others. They had smashed the window pane of the second floor of the taller building. The window was the same size as the previous one but unlike it, it was at a height. Everyone had to be hauled up to enter it and jump inside the building.

I was totally startled at how their appearance had messed my head earlier. I stood face to face with my prejudice and I made a silent promise not to judge people based on their appearance.

The team had to lift every single person and push them through the smashed window into the building. They had to lift more than 200 people one after the other without any rest.

When they were lifting women, I noticed there was no difference in their attitude. No body cared whether she was a young girl or an old woman.

In the chaos, a woman's salwar (lower) loosened and dropped. She was almost naked but no one bothered about it. She was also lifted by the men decently and helped to safety. Afterwards, one man picked up her salwar and threw it to her. I am sure no man had any vulgar sexual thoughts

---

[6] *saviour*

in his mind at that time. All corruption and vulgarity house in a person's mind when he is safe and satiated.

When our turn came, we realised that watching other people being thrown was one thing, but undergoing the same hair-raising experience was quite another.

One after the other, I saw Anshu, Radhu, Anju, Neha, Aarav, Manoj being thrown into the window like balls. But when those two men picked me up a strange sort of fear gripped me.

I thought what would happen if while getting thrown I rolled back and fell into the water, or what if I didn't land safely in the room or got bruised by the sharp glass edges?

These nerve-racking thoughts almost killed my courage, but I held my breath and hoped all would go well.

Why am I using the word 'thrown' instead of helped? Because that is exactly what was happening. The window was at a height and time was precious. The volunteers were focused on getting everyone through it as fast as possible. So they unceremoniously heaved and threw us all through the window like one would throw bags or briefcases. They couldn't afford to care whether the person got hurt. Speed was all that mattered. We had turned into non-living things.

I saw some people had managed to bring along small suitcases and bags. I almost applauded them for their passion for material things. And for making as much effort to save their stuff as they did to save themselves.

How could they do it?

Forget risking their own lives in holding a suitcase in one hand and the railing with the other, the volunteers had repeatedly requested people not to bring along heavy things. The roof could give way any moment jeopardizing the entire evacuation process. Did they not think about the people who were behind them?

And yet they had brought their luggage.

I am sure if they had seen a man drowning like I had, they wouldn't have taken the warnings so casually.

This is the human nature I suppose. We don't take warnings seriously. We are always very sure that nothing untoward will happen to us.

I wondered what they carried in those bags. What was more alluring to them than precious life? How and when did love of money and material things become the ruling passion of human life? I simply could not shake off this question.

Our kids, like other young people, went through the ordeal with dauntless courage and unquestioning obedience. In addition to that, I don't know how they managed to retain their spirits and crack jokes. They lent an ear to every desperate call for help they heard. I saw Parth and Anshu diverting the attention of scared and weepy kids who were beyond their mothers' efforts to calm them. They started playing cricket with a boy who was howling, making him forget the trauma for a while.

May God bless all who helped us cross to safety.

At length, the first level of our game of survival was complete.

CHAPTER 2

June 1998

"Kashish! Why is Parth crying again? Have you done something to him?" roared his father at the top of his voice.

"Papa, you don't know what he did! I slapped him, and now he is crying and screaming his head off!"

"But why did you hit him? Why can't you be nice to your brother?"

"He has thrown my binoculars in the pond," sobbed Kashish.

"I didn't throw them. They slipped from my hands," explained little Parth.

"But why did you touch them? How many times have I told you to keep away from my things?"

"I was just looking at them and they fell into the water," Parth clarified innocently.

"And who told you to touch them? I will give you a whack if you come near my things again," thundered Kashish.

"Papa! Papa! *Bhaiya*[7] is beating me," yelled Parth.

"Aww! My baby! Come, let me give you a hug. I will scold Kashi," consoled Papa.

He reasoned with Kashish, "Kashi *beta*[8], it happened accidentally. He didn't mean to throw it. Leave him alone now."

"Papa, you always take his side and never support me. I want my binoculars back, else I will throw him into the same pond."

"Relax Kashi! I will get you a new one. Now be friends with him."

"First get me a new one!" Kashi was adamant.

"You know nothing is available now in Kashmir. No shop is open. We can't even buy food! When we return to Delhi, I will get you a new one...better than this pair."

"No, I want it now!" Kashish howled louder.

And so it continued. Both boys, as usual, drove their father up the wall as he tried to pacify and reason with them.

It was a day full of life and laughter thirteen years ago at Nishat Garden in Kashmir. I was visiting with my husband and our two little feisty and adorable kids.

---

[7]   *Brother*

[8]   *Son*

Anil, my husband, 10-year-old Kashish, 4-year-old Parth and I were on a pilgrimage to Mata Vaishno Devi temple at Jammu in the year 1998.

During the trip we heard that the Indian government had given tourists permission to travel to the Kashmir valley. This had happened after a very long period of unrest in the region.

The wars between India and Pakistan in 1947, 1965, 1971 and the Kargil conflict over the possession of Kashmir had killed thousands of people on both sides. The conflict had taken its toll and entry of tourists in the valley had been restricted.

When Anil heard that tourists could enter Kashmir, he was ecstatic. He had always desired to visit the 'heaven-on-earth' and he wasn't about to let the chance slip by. He immediately made arrangements for a visit and we hired a taxi. All four of us were very excited, as going to Kashmir was rare in those days.

On the way we had to cross several dangerous areas. We saw no tourists at all throughout, only Indian army trucks, jeeps and *jawans*[9].

Even local people weren't to be seen out of their homes. No children were playing on the streets, no restaurants were open, no signs of normal life anywhere.

---

[9]   *Soldier*

39

A strange sort of fear hung in the air.

Our taxi driver, even after searching for many hours, couldn't find any vegetarian restaurant open. He told us that there used to be many, but due to terrorist activities every single eating joint was shut.

All through the journey, we ate only chips and biscuits, which we had brought from Jammu.

En route, we realised army jeeps were following us. Instead of local people, all we saw was the BSF (Border Security Force) everywhere. They were very warm, courteous and ready to assist us if we needed anything.

They guarded us like a mother guards her babies. In fact, they had been very surprised to see us in the valley. We were almost the first tourist group to enter Kashmir so soon after the government had relaxed norms.

They were by our side constantly and were delighted to talk to us. They shared stories about the risks and the dangers they faced everyday and despite it all, how they loved to work for the nation. They confided in us that they were relieved to see us in Kashmir as they were seeing new faces in Srinagar after a very long time. In fact, they seemed happier than us that tourists were beginning to visit Kashmir.

While travelling, we saw sacks full of sand placed at the entrance of most houses. When we enquired why it was so, the driver explained that they were there to help people dodge bullets and ensure the safety of all who lived in the house. He also told us stories about bomb blasts, which were very normal in those days.

It became very clear to us that there was no security of life anywhere. The beautiful tales of the vale we had heard since childhood seemed like unreal fantasies. On the contrary, the place was in a ruinous state.

Our taxi driver took us to Pintail Houseboat on Dal Lake and arranged a room for us. The owners were simple Kashmiris who were overjoyed on seeing tourists. They offered us the best room on the boat and served us with much love and affection. We stayed there for almost a week.

They prepared delicious vegetarian meals with utmost care and whenever we went out sightseeing, they packed something for us saying, "Sir, you won't find anything to eat on the way as all shops and restaurants have been closed for security reasons."

Their void eyes reflected the anguish of living in a place with omnipresent danger. Being the original inhabitants of Kashmir, they couldn't think of moving out to set up a new life in any other state of India. They were trapped and had no choice but to bear the prolonged conflict.

Though the BSF had been protecting them from dawn to dusk, the bad blood between India and Pakistan had poisoned the trust between the army and the public. The conflict had taken its toll.

During our week there, we went to see all the famous places. Nishat and Shalimar Gardens, Chashme Shahi, the famous cricket bat factories, apple orchards, and the Shankaracharya temple. Despite the all-pervasive gloom, we had a wonderful time and relished every moment.

Generally, when one visits tourist spots, one meets other groups of tourists from different parts of the country. But in Kashmir our only friends were army *jawans*[10] who provided us with not only security but also company.

Though every place we visited had army units stationed there, and no piece of the land was totally safe, I never felt too troubled because I was with my partner. He made me feel safe and protected in the most insecure place. He was like a shield and his presence enveloped my kids and me in an embrace of serenity and security.

Just how protected I felt in his presence, I realised only on the darkest day of my life.

3rd March 2001

6 p.m.

Somebody at the door was pressing on the doorbell with all their might.

Getting irritated at such persistence, I opened the door to find Amit and Manit, my elder sister Ginni's sons, there.

---

[10] *Soldier*

They said, "*Maasi*[11] get ready. We are going to Kailash Nursing Home. *Mausaji*[12] is admitted there."

Shocked, I replied, "No, Anil has gone to Lucknow for Khaatu Shyamji *jaagran*[13]."

Manit replied, "No, *Maasi*[14]. His stomach started aching at the railway station. So he went to *Mamaji's*[15] clinic from there."

In the meanwhile, my elder sisters Ginni and Meena also arrived and we all drove to the hospital.

I found both sides of my family already gathered there.

As soon as I entered Anil's ward, instead of feeling relieved to see me, he admonished me affectionately, "Renu, why have you come here? I'm absolutely fine. Only a little pain in the stomach that'll be okay in a day or two. Nothing to worry!"

He knew how I hated going to hospitals. He didn't want me to panic. He was all loving and caring and thinking more about me even when he was lying on a hospital bed.

---

[11] Aunt (Mother's sister)

[12] Aunt (Mother's sister)

[13] A religious wake where devotees stay awake all night singing devotional songs

[14] Aunt (Mother's sister)

[15] Uncle (Mother's brother)

I broke down and said, "OK! Just let me talk to the doctor" and rushed out of the room.

Dr. Anil, my dear cousin, was there. The only doctor in our entire *khandan*[16] without whose consultation none of us dares to move ahead when ill or injured——what hospital to go, which surgeon to choose and which medicine to take? Everyone, even today, follows his advice. He has our absolute faith. For 25 years, he has served the entire family with utmost devotion and we hold him in high regard.

All stood silent around him. He finally spoke, "We'll shift Anil *jijaji* to Sir Ganga Ram Hospital tomorrow morning as his reports are not too good. His pancreas and heart are not functioning properly."

We were stunned! How could this happen so suddenly?

On being informed of the shift, my husband asked my cousin, "What about Agarsen Hospital? That's more affordable. Ganga Ram is beyond my budget."

Even in that emergency, he was more worried about the bills than his health. We belonged to a middle class family where every penny meant a lot. He knew going to Ganga Ram would not only drain our resources but could put us in debt.

I assured him, "Both my *jijajis* are here to help us. The younger one is taking care of the money. You don't worry about it. My jewellery can be sold and we have some

---

16 *clan*

savings too. If needed, we also have a good flat. You are more important than anything else. You be OK and we can handle all else."

My elder *jijaji's* financial position was not very sound in those days, but he stood by me round the clock like a father, always there to ensure I did not fall apart.

My younger *jijaji* was very well off. The very first day he told me, "Renu, you don't have to worry about a single penny. Get Anil the best of medical facilities. I have enough properties and if needed, I'll sell one or two of them to arrange for whatever amount is needed. But his treatment should not suffer." He was a firm believer that money can always be earned, but life, once gone, cannot.

Anil was taken to Ganga Ram on 5thMarch 2001 at 10 a.m.

My younger *jijaji* kept his promise. He would deposit the advance in the hospital account daily. Not even once did the staff have to remind us to pay up or replenish a lowering balance. He proved to be *Kuber*[17] at the time we needed most, and he did it right to the end.

Since the time Anil was admitted to the ICU, a very large number of his friends, relatives and neighbours queued up to enquire about his health, which unfortunately deteriorated with every passing hour.

---

[17] *Lord of wealth*

Anil was a very social person who enjoyed a very good reputation in the *mandals*[18] of Khaatu Shyamji in Delhi. Almost all affluent Aggarwals (*Baniya*[19] community) were members of these *mandals*[20]. He was adored and admired by almost all because of his warmth and geniality.

Yet, there were those who envied him too. But he hardly cared for negativity. All he wanted was to sing *bhajans*[21] for Shyamji. He had undying faith on Shyam Baba and his own guruji Shri Jaishankar Chaudhary of Calcutta.

Anil's favourite verse was——

"*Maanga hai maine shyam se vardaan ek hi,*[22]
Teri kripa bani rahe jab tak hai zindagi."[23]

And Shyam Baba repaid him duly.

Only two months back, on 31st December 2000, Anil had organised Delhi's grandest *jaagran*[24] in Talkatora Stadium all on his own. This massive stadium was bedecked in flowers and the fragrance hung in the air mingling with

---

[18] *a group of people who organize religious events for the community*
[19] *A caste usually associated with business community*
[20] *a group of people who organize religious events for the community*
[21] *devotional songs*
[22] *I have asked for only one thing from Shyam,*
[23] *Shower your blessing on me all my life*
[24] *A religious wake where devotees stay awake all night singing devotional songs*

mesmerising scents of *itr[25]. A large number of devotees and celebrities from all over India had attended it.

The grand event was so flawlessly organised that everyone was awestruck. "How did a single soul manage such a miracle," all whispered.

But there were some who turned green with envy. They were people from competitive *mandals[26] who were always ready to take a dig at him because of his rising popularity.

But I knew that his success was the outcome of his ceaseless efforts and the grace of God. He had invested every minute of an entire year to put up a show, the likes of which had never been seen before and one that would reverberate in memory for years to come. Many *bhakti[27] and news channels covered the *jaagran[28]. Anil had reached the pinnacle of success and had accomplished a long cherished goal.

We were still basking in the success of the event when life took a flip-side turn. Once a sturdily built man, Anil now lay helpless in the ICU. His body was not able to pass urine. So the doctors strictly forbade him from drinking any water.

His body was swelling up rapidly because of metabolic disorders and he remained in a hypercritical condition for four days.

---

[25] scent
[26] *a group of people who organize religious events for the community*
[27] *Devotional/God Channels*
[28] *A religious wake where devotees stay awake all night singing devotional songs*

During those four days, whenever he was conscious, he would say, "*'Renu, mujhe Limca pilaa de, ye doctors tou mujhe maar hi daalenge.*"[29]

He begged for water. Even a single drop would do, he cried. But it wasn't allowed. I would just mumble, "Let me bring some, you please lie still," and leave the room. But I never could keep my promise. I couldn't quench the thirst of my dying husband. How would I ever compensate for this grave sin I wondered.

Hiding my tears, I would come out of the room, embrace my mom and my mother-in-law, and just cry. Both women had lost their husbands only a few years ago so they knew the trauma I was going through. They never left me alone and would console me, "*'Beta, sab theek ho jayega.*"[30] During that week, they went to temples, met astrologers and *'pandits*[31], and did whatever was suggested by anyone.

Still Anil did not come around and continued to suffer.

On the fifth morning, when I entered the ICU, I could just not bear the sight. Nurses had tied Anil's hands and legs firmly to the bed and had taped his mouth so he couldn't shout for water. His body had almost doubled in size and his lips were turning blue.

---

[29]   *Renu, please get me some Limca. These doctors will kill me.*

[30]   *Child, all will be well*

[31]   *priests*

I pleaded with my cousin, "*Bhaiya*[32], what use is your medical science? You can transplant all body parts but is there no way to drain urine from his body?"

He hugged me and tried to console me. "Renu, don't worry. Doctors are doing all they can to save Anil."

I could sense his voice breaking and see tears in his wife's eyes. No doubt, they were hiding the truth from me. A voice screamed inside me that something was terribly wrong.

Just then Vijay *chachaji*[33] tapped on my shoulder, "*Beta*[34], how is Anil now? Is he recovering? Where are Kashish and Parth?"

I told him the kids were at my sister's house.

He continued, "Is any LIC instalment of Anil's due? Go home and check. If yes, tell me, I'll deposit it today only."

Sheepishly and with some annoyance I said, "I don't know anything about his financial and legal documents."

But he persisted. Subhash *chachaji*[35] also joined him and they questioned me repeatedly about the LIC policy. I was upset and getting irritated over their focus on money even in such critical hours.

---

[32] *Brother*

[33] *Uncle (father's brother)*

[34] *Son*

[35] *Uncle (father's brother)*

Not having dealt with any finances ever, I couldn't fathom their fatherly foresight. They had faced up to the fact that anything could happen to Anil and were trying to secure my future. I realised and regretted my lack of judgement only a year later.

On the sixth day, Anil went into coma.

And then it started—ECG, dialysis, ventilators and a whole host of procedures. I was seeing my man dying piece by piece.

But I knew no peace. Every moment I searched for any shred of strength left within me. I had to steel myself for the unimagined calamities waiting ahead.

And they arrived soon enough.

The innumerable tests and procedures were followed by a string of failures—pancreas, kidney, lungs and finally the heart.

On 20th March 2001 at 10:20 a.m. Anil breathed his last, leaving my kids and me alone in this world.

Fortune left its cherished child
and bestowed her with malice piled,
And she was with misfortunes piled!

With him, something broke within

I had to come to terms with the fact that the man whose presence was the reality of our lives would now not be seen anywhere.

The first 17 days after his passing, the house was full with hoards of people who came for the final rituals. Everyone was beside themselves with grief.

But even in the midst of their sorrow, my in-laws suggested that I should get re-married.

My mother-in-law reasoned, "I don't want Renu to suffer alone like me. I know how people look at a widow and try to take advantage. It is a pretty long life and everyone needs a partner. So we must try to find a suitable match for her at the earliest."

My own family was amazed at her words. Only a few days ago she had lost her eldest son, but she was still concerned about me. She wanted good fortune for his family. What a lady! How could she be so genuine and kind hearted?

I am really privileged to have tied the matrimonial knot with her son. She was much more than a mother to me.

What does a man mean to his family? It can be described well only by those who have lost the man of their house and pass every second sans the essence of life and under a dreaded state of mind.

After Anil, everything——the house, the relatives, the street, the work, the office, the entire world remained the same, but the absence of that one man sucked the aroma of life from us, rendering everything tasteless and lifeless.

My husband, the father of my kids, the man of our house had always been full of love, laughter and life. He was passionate and adventurous and the life of every gathering.

I asked myself, "Where has the man disappeared whose love was the essence of our being? A man who showered extreme concern and love on all three of us? A husband and a father who would sacrifice his comforts for the sake of his family so that they could stay stress-free?"

I remember every moment spent in his beloved company.

They will remain buried deep inside my heart like my most precious possessions.

CHAPTER 3

Now once again I was visiting Kashmir with Parth and two of my nieces' families.

The preparation and packing for this trip had begun like they do for all vacations. Shopping for branded things—jeans, trousers, t-shirts, shoes, belts, bags, cosmetics and god knows what else—went on till the eleventh hour. We packed our suitcases with great enthusiasm and headed for Srinagar.

2nd September 2014

Ours was a 6 a.m. flight. My elder son, Kashish, dropped us to the airport. While bidding him goodbye, I couldn't have imagined in my wildest dreams that soon I would be so badly yearning to see his face.

At the airport, the party of nine greeted each other and asked what the others had brought for breakfast. After boarding the Jet Airways flight and settling in, Anju opened her tiffin box and offered mouth-watering *dhokla*[36] to all.

---

[36] *A Gujrati delicacy*

Oh, the wonderful taste! It was made by Anju's sister-in-law, Meenu, and was cooked to perfection. I wolfed down my share and more, and then shamelessly announced only I would eat all the remaining pieces. Thankfully for the others, the quantity Anju had brought outstripped my greed.

Apart from *dhokla*[37], she had also brought *poori*[38] and karela sabzi. Neha passed around *namkeens*[39], biscuits and cold drinks. Next, the vegetable biryani I had brought was thoroughly enjoyed by all. The breakfast was finally rounded off with many packets of popcorn. By the time we had gluttoned through all the food, it was time to land at Srinagar.

As soon as we stepped out of the plane, cool breeze greeted us. What a relief from the scorching heat of Delhi, a city that turns into Rajasthan in the hot months of April to August.

We loaded our luggage and ourselves into the Tempo Traveller, which we had booked from Delhi. Everyone was agog with excitement and was anticipating a vacation packed with adventure.

As soon as we left the airport, we realised Neha had left her iPad in the plane. Her husband, our dear Manoj, lost his temper and screamed at her for not being vigilant about her belongings. It took the entire gang to control him.

---

[37] *A Gujrati delicacy*
[38] *Deep fried and puffed up bread*
[39] *salty snack*

Sanjay, the cool-headed one, took Manoj back into the airport to try and recover the iPad. The rest of us waited in the Tempo with little hope but with fingers crossed. To our great astonishment, they came back with the tablet in their hands. The airport personnel had been very cooperative and helped them retrieve it.

Extremely surprised at our luck in getting the tablet back, we furthered our trip and headed to the houseboat where we had to stay overnight. We were supposed to be tired as no one had slept the previous night, but our spirits were high. You can credit the magical air of Kashmir for nobody wanting to stay indoors. All had their hearts set on sightseeing. Every moment was precious and we wanted to soak in the bewitching beauty of every corner of the valley.

But first we ate lunch in the vicinity of the houseboat. The spectacular scene at the Dal Lake, especially the *shikaras*[40] floating on the lake, charmed us. There was something delicious in the air.

The sugar-tongued shopkeepers at the corner of the lake tried enticing us to buy jackets, purses, caps, etc. But nobody was in the mood to shop so early, so we ignored them. Instead, we went to see the enchanting Nishat and Shalimar Gardens. We were extremely excited, including the driver Hasan. In only half an hour, he brought us to the gates of the Nishat.

---

[40] *houseboat*

But as soon as I stepped out of the Tempo and looked around, all my joy vanished and I was hit by a deep sense of despair. I was suddenly engulfed in a storm of sorrow.

But I managed to drag myself after the others.

Inside the garden, everything seemed as still as it had been a decade ago. The same tall trees were standing firm, the vines twined around thicker branches, and the flowers graced the garden in handsome hues.

It's brilliant beauty beggared description. But the stunning sight depressed me rather than lifting my spirits. I retired into a lonely corner to cry my heart out for a few minutes, as it grew impossible to pretend to be happy anymore.

Merry memories of the bygone aeon with Anil in Nishat Garden started rewinding. That wonderful time, those magical moments whose fragrance I carried deep in my heart overwhelmed me. I slipped into a dreamy state finding myself back in my husband's era.

My mind flew to the moment Anil, me, Kashish and Parth had been sitting under a tall pine tree in this very garden, sharing our lunch with the few army *jawans* who had become buddies with us.

Kashish, eyeing the guns they were carrying, had asked, "Sir, please let me hold this gun…just once." The solider refused, explaining, "No, dear boy. It is very dangerous and you can't hold it."

But Kashish pestered and the *jawan* kept refusing. This went on till they settled on Kashish just touching the gun but not holding it in his hands.

That compromise satisfied the kid and amused everyone. The *jawans* also said that they were relishing those light moments after a long and tense *yuga*[41].

Ten years later, I sat alone feeling Anil's presence everywhere. I recalled the photo sessions: army men clicking our pictures wherever we requested––in front of the flower patches, near the fountains or on the staircases. Being the first visitors to the valley, we were being treated like celebrities by the BSF.

My mind slipped into another memory recalling how the radiance of the 'paradise-on-earth' did not much impress our children who were busy in their own games.

I remembered young Parth kicking Kashish who had lost a bet with his kid brother. But when Parth kicked him more than the decided number of times, a fight broke out. Kashish ran after Parth yelling, "Now I won't spare you! I will kick you double the number of times."

And Parth ran to his father, "Papa! Save me! *Bhaiya* is threatening to kick me ten times."

Anil warned Kashish, "Let him be, Kasha. He is your little brother. He won't break the rules next time."

---

[41] *mythological age (unit of time)*

But adamant Kashish screamed louder, "No way! I will have my revenge."

Anil, though protective about Parth, was thrilled to see Kashish as naughty as he himself had been in his childhood. He always said, "Parth is the exact opposite of me and Kashish. How come he is so sweet natured and decent? He must have inherited these quaint qualities from his mother. Kashish and I simply don't belong to this strange and serene category. There is no fun in not being funny."

Those moments, those words, that love, that part of our life––where did it go? Why was he snatched away from us? Where is he now? In what form? Is he among the stars in the vast sky? Is he looking at us from above?

How desperate and bound he must be feeling at not being able to join us. He must be struggling to free himself from the clutches of the Almighty. Many a time, I sensed that if I stretched my hand, I would be able to touch him and hold him. But he was just in my thoughts, away from our world.

When my thoughts wandered back to the present and I found myself standing alone, a very different person from what I had been 10 years ago. Hardships the three of us had to face after him had entirely changed our personalities.

The flashback receded just as the past had. My little son Parth had turned into a handsome young boy of 19 years and the awfully naughty Kashish had completed 26 winters. He had mellowed with the years. His playfulness too had abandoned him with his father.

Nishat garden though was the same as it had been a decade ago. Only the mortal soul that gave it so much charm had disappeared from this earth after enjoying its assigned breaths.

In fact, nature doesn't change till we human beings try our dirty hands on it to mar its marvelousness. It was the same with Nishat. Kashmir outside of it had transformed; the garden was as gorgeous as ever.

But unlike nature, we change. We have to change.

Time has wings
It slips from our hands every moment!
This passing moment too,
In the next moment, will become the past.

After Anil, we were left behind to initiate a new life with new characters in a new world that was strange and scary. We had to keep moving even though every moment we cried over our irreparable loss. We did not stop breathing, eating, living, weeping, laughing and following the daily routine though. Except, we had transformed from a blossoming family into a withered one.

The first three months after the tragedy, we kept shifting between Ginni *di's*[42] and Meena *di's*[43] homes. They were most attentive to all our needs and ready to do anything to soothe us.

---

[42] *respectful epithet for elder sister*
[43] *respectful epithet for elder sister*

All my sisters busied themselves in trying to find a suitable match for me including Raj *di*[44], my eldest sister who lived in Tiptur, a small beautiful city 250 kms away from Bengaluru.

She would tell my mother, "We'll get Renu remarried. I'll adopt Kashish and look after him very well. Nobody has to worry about him. We just have to focus on Renu's life. Don't get hung up on whether the man belongs to our community or is a South Indian. I know many good families around Bengaluru and I'll try my best to find a match. I cannot see her in this state of distress."

Raj *di*[45] had always been very fond of me as for her I was like her own child. I was just six months old when she had been married.

She would burst into tears on seeing me in white or light coloured clothes.

While both my families were trying to look for a match, my mother was dead against my remarrying. "No, this will not be right. No one can replace my son-in-law. Such a bhakt's wife should pay him a tribute by staying with his name. God and he will look after the family."

My sorrows deepened on seeing her in tears, always praying. She counselled, "*Beta*, time will be very hard now onwards. You'll have to undergo very critical stages. But be strong for

---

[44]   *respectful epithet for elder sister*
[45]   *respectful epithet for elder sister*

your kids. You have to play the dual role of a mother and a father. I'm sure Shyam Baba will certainly help you through your hard phase."

Her words strengthened me. But I wondered how many grim sins I had committed in my past births that I became the source of endless grief for both mothers in their old age.

And how ironical it was! While my mother-in-law desperately wished to get me re-married, my own mother stood firmly against the idea. Both had precise plans for me.

My father had expired one-and-a-half years back on 14th October, 1999. It was some consolation to me that he didn't have to see this dark chapter of his daughter's life. He had always seen Anil joyous, singing in big gatherings, appreciated and loved by all.

He always said, "Anil is a charmer. He has brought incredible glory to our family. We are very proud of him."

I thank God my father left for his heavenly abode with a glorious image of Anil intact in his mind.

But everyone else's life came to a standstill...focussed only on me! Every other day, relatives and friends would come over to my place to suggest what I should do next.

Some said, "You should sell this house, buy a smaller place and with the rest of the amount you can lead your life peacefully."

Others opined, "You should look for a job because you will need a regular income to run the house."

Yet others suggested, "The only way is to reduce your expenses so that you can save something."

Many said, "Why don't you sell your jewellery and deposit the amount in the bank and live off the interest."

There were many more suggestions and ideas. But no unanimous decision on how I should proceed.

Everybody produced vague ideas not telling me how exactly to execute them. The bigger problem was if I told anyone that I wouldn't be able to take their advice, they took offence, shrugged and would go around grumbling, "It is useless to advise her. She will do whatever she wants. She doesn't care about what we say." They would then leave, never to return again.

And if I dared to offer counter arguments to why their suggestions lacked merit, for e.g. selling the house, then they would feel as if I had insulted them and would start speaking ill of me.

You know what happens in cases like mine, where the female doesn't have her father, father-in-law, husband, elder brother-in-law or any older male figure who can set up her life for her? Hundreds line up to yap about what she should do, but no one actually helps.

The woman not only loses her husband but her security, respect, confidence and most importantly freedom of speech, thought and action. A post-graduate person, me, immediately became a moron, incompetent of having any wise thoughts.

The number of visitors dwindled with each passing day. Supposed well wishers started giving me a wide berth. Only Ginni *di*[46] and *jijaji* were with me during those challenging days. While they couldn't help me with money due to their own financial issues, they stood by me and supported all my decisions.

I was clear I would never take any money from anybody. In fact, after Anil's death, many members of Shyam *mandals* proposed they would deposit a good amount of money for our future since Anil had done so much for these *mandals*. But we declined their kind offer.

All I wanted was someone to guide me properly. To tell me, "Renu, you do this, and this is how you go about it. We are there with you no matter what the outcome." And in case my attempts at following their suggestions failed, then not to blame or castigate me.

My ears craved to hear some soothing words of support, but I heard only criticism.

Gradually, people forgot my tragedy and got busy with their own lives. I also stopped opening up about my problems with everyone and opted to solve them on my own.

---

[46] *respectful epithet for elder sister*

It was not an easy decision. In fact, it was a Herculean task.

Just as a beggar has no buddies
We, once God's favourites, were also left with no friends!

I had to initiate a lonely and backbreaking journey of transforming from a pampered homemaker whose partner took care of all finances and affairs outside the house, to a single woman who would now have to shoulder thousands of chores outside and inside the home singlehandedly.

The first and foremost question was what to do to earn money? Where to go? Whom to ask? What kind of work and how? I had hardly any experience of doing anything except managing my home and children. Anyone I came across in those days, I would ask if they could help me get a job.

Then one day, an acquaintance, Mr. Raheja, offered to set up an interview for the job of a receptionist in a good company. He knew the director of the company very well.

This was my very first step outside my home into the world of careers and money making.

I was visibly nervous and it clearly showed on my face.

The director, Mr. Kapoor, asked, "Renu, does the AC of your car cool properly?"

I was amazed at the irrelevant question, but answered anyway, "Yes Sir, it works very well."

It was only much later, while speaking to a friend that I realised he was using the car and AC question as a barometer to check on my financial and social status. He was trying to gauge just how much trouble I was in.

Next he asked, "Do you know how to work on a computer?"

Although the chances of getting the job depended on how I answered every query, I responded truthfully, "No Sir, but I will learn only in a few days."

He said, "OK. But the job I am offering you on Mr. Raheja's reference would require you to travel for a day or two either to Agra or Jaipur. Is that acceptable to you?"

I became very excited as the chances of landing the job seemed quite good and I hastily replied, "Yes Sir, I can manage. I'll drop my kids at my sister's place."

Staring straight into my eyes he said, "With me?"

I started trembling in astonishment at his statement. It seemed as if I had heard something wrong and murmured, "What Sir?"

He very casually repeated the same, "Will you be able to go out of station for a day or two with me?"

Aghast, I stood up and said, "No Sir!" I bolted out of the room and broke into tears.

The job was lost.

In my car, I just kept crying and wondering, "What will I tell Kashish?"

He was the only soul with whom I shared all that happened during the day. He knew that I had gone for an interview in that particular company on Mr. Raheja's reference. Kashish knew Mr. Raheja had great respect for his father and believed sincerely that he would surely get his mother a good job.

We had indeed been very optimistic about this opportunity. It was supposed to improve our financial condition. Kashish and I were aware that our situation was so unstable that I often did not know where the expenses for the next day would come from.

Such humiliating experiences were absolutely new to me. Till then I had been in a very protective environment. But now my destiny had brought me into an alien world where security seemed like a far away rainbow.

I reached home in a state where I didn't have to mention anything to Kasha. He understood something was wrong and didn't put up any questions. When did my boy become such a master of judging situations?

Such experiences did not end with that one man. They continued. So did their impact.

This meeting in particular had shattered me. I felt betrayed and I no longer knew whom to trust. Recalling all the awkward questions from the interview in discussions with a friend, I slowly realised all the information he had been trying to get out of me. I felt small and totally insulted.

In this office or that, for any kind of job I was referred to, whether the interviewer was young, middle aged or old, I had to confront the same sort of annoying questions sooner or later. Only the words differed, but the motto was crystal clear.

Gradually, my bitter experiences made me smart enough to read between the lines. The insinuations and propositions on account of being a single woman became evident. But I never reacted aggressively as I was too timid. I did not want to face any complications, so kept mum.

Though it was not so simple for me to earn money in a world where anyone who offered me a job was ready to tear me apart bodily and emotionally, I did not give up.

With time I understood that now existed no real relations, no real friends, no real well wishers.

To every man I was just a woman! Most men I encountered looked at me hawk-eyed, waiting for a chance to take advantage of me.

It was solely up to me whether to succumb to their advances, make compromises and provide a hassle-free, comfortable life to my kids––a life that would shrivel my soul. Or to choose a life full of struggle, stress and loneliness, but one that would satisfy my soul.

I opted for the latter––every moment full of struggle, but laced with one faith, "Yes, we can make it. How won't God help us if we are on the right path?"

I took the one less travelled by, and that has made all the difference.

These lines from 'The Road Not Taken' by Robert Frost inspired me and directed my life to the right path.

I believed and taught my kids––

Himmate banda tou madad-ae-khuda
Naa himmate banda tou bezaar khuda

As an earnest newcomer to the field of money-making, I tried hands at several jobs––private tuitions, event management, selling suit materials, Tupperware goods and many more.

I went ahead with whatever work I got. I never said no to any work. In fact, I couldn't afford to say no. My only motive was to have in my hands at least Rs. 200–300 by every evening so that we could meet our basic minimum needs.

Like a maniac, I would keep thinking about where my next gig would come from.

Each passing day appeared indispensably long, exhausting both flesh and mind, and every single vein in my body.

It was not just finances that hassled me. I was encountering problems with relatives and friends too. I had trouble understanding their changing moods and their concerns for me. Their sole focus was on practical aspects of my life and not on my emotional wellbeing.

Some stayed, but many left.

My dear cousin sisters-in-law, Rashmi *di*[47] and Sangeeta *di*[48] did a lot for us. Sudha chachi and Ginni *di*[49] never failed to visit on the festivals and other celebrations like birthdays. They would come with bags full of needed grocery and stationery items. Their visits made us feel still loved and wanted.

Apart from them, nobody showed interest in us without some self-interest or expectation, leaving only the three of us for us.

One day, my husband's friend came to my house with his wife. During the conversation he said, "How brave Anil was! He never cried when his father died, who passed away when Anil was sixteen leaving behind three young children and his wife. I remember how Anil worked hard day and night and took great care of his brothers, his sister and his mother. He was indeed a gem and set an example of just how wonderfully one can raise a family!"

---

[47] *respectful epithet for elder sister*

[48] *respectful epithet for elder sister*

[49] *respectful epithet for elder sister*

While recounting this story, he suddenly said, "Renu, you have to have heart now and it's your turn to repeat whatever he did. I agree it is not easy to raise two small kids. If you need any assistance, tell me. I'm always there for your welfare."

The second he called me 'Renu', I was stunned and covered with humiliation. I seethed, "How can he call me by my name instead of bhabhi?"

I had never heard anybody addressing me by my name in my in-laws family even if the person was elder to me. Everybody had always showered much respect and always called me bhabhi. How could he now insult me by using my name? And why did he do so?

Words always have consequences. They either heal or hurt.

He had come to heal my wounds but just the word 'Renu' hurt me deeply. It showed me that my status had changed. I had become simple 'Renu', without any respected epithet to grace my name––no didi, no bhabhi, no Mrs. Mittal.

Do these relationships end with the end of the man?

This was the first shock I received from an old acquaintance who started building a new relationship with me instead of respecting the previous one.

Moreover, the way he offered assistance didn't convince me at all. I could smell something fishy in his lascivious tone, which got under my skin. And though I wanted to question him, the adversity of time didn't let me utter a word and I kept sitting like a statue throughout his visit.

After he left, I wondered what are these relationships we swear by day and night? They change with a single stroke of fate.

And nothing is permanent. Not love, not emotions, not feelings. My husband had planned to stay with me forever, to settle in Goa after we were 65. He said he would never leave me. Those promises too were now mere words.

With his leaving us, other men did not miss a heartbeat before trying to entice me using similar phrases. Perhaps all words are just sugary baits that are thrown by people to entrap others for their own selfish needs.

But despite tragic loss and crumbling relationships, everyone has to move on. I recall what Shakespeare has said:

All the world's a stage
And all the men and women merely players:
They have their exits and their entrances;
And one man in his time plays many parts,
His acts being seven ages.

Shakespeare so wisely compares the world to a stage on which the drama of life is enacted. Every one exhibits their puppetry skills performing the prescribed role. Then they take leave from this planet never to be seen again just as Anil had. He played his brief part and departed from the stage of life.

Actors like my kids and me were left behind to keep lamenting our loss but to no avail. Whosoever disappears from this world can by no means be made to reappear. The situation can never be reversed. Whatever God has done, cannot be undone. People have to find ways to go ahead, without their loved and lost ones.

As we did though feeling constantly that we wouldn't be able to, days progressed and so did we.

Suddenly, I heard Parth calling me loudly, "Mumma! Come here! We are waiting for you to take a group snap." He came to the corner I was sitting in and took me with him.

I am one of those fortunate beings in the world who are blessed with the most affectionate kids. My children are always around to do anything to make their mother happy.

Parth never leaves me alone and keeps a watch on me, especially when I look a little serious.

He looked at me with concern again and asked, "Are you crying Mom? Why are there tears in your eyes?"

I said, "No, I'm absolutely okay!"

But he persisted. "I can see tears. Tell me, why you are standing here alone and crying?"

Despite my repeated denials, he didn't believe me I was OK. He gave me a tender peck on my cheeks and pulled me along to where everyone else was enjoying.

I gave my head a shake and let my emotions pass.

Once again I mingled with the group and their laughter and merry making.

CHAPTER 4

7th September 2014

11 a.m.

We reached the taller wing of CH2 after putting our lives at risk, only to find complete mayhem there.

Small children were wailing away –– may be they were hungry. Others were bickering and squabbling. Their hassled parents were trying to pacify them by making false promises of getting them this thing or that.

But hunger can never be satiated by words alone; it takes over and overwhelms. People were unable to arrange for even tiny bits of food for their starving kids.

The top floor was crammed with local Kashmiris who had reached there just like us from adjacent houses to save themselves from the cruel tyranny of water. More than 300 people, including our group, had taken shelter in that wing of CH2.

The locals were sitting numb, bereft of all thoughts and possessions. They were watching their hard earned money, jewellery, land, property, cars, TVs, computers, refrigerators, books, identity cards, passports, school and college certificates, medals, and so much more, all being washed away by the deluge. They couldn't lift a finger or do anything to save any of it. Their hands were tied.

The most surprising thing was that they were utterly silent, not discussing their lost assets at all. May be shock had turned them speechless, or may be they knew lamenting about all they had lost would be of no help.

In a corner by themselves sat a family––an old man, his wife and a daughter of around 18 years. The mother was shedding tears and the daughter was trying her best to console the older woman.

Every now and then the man, who was lame, was seen enquiring something from other people. He was hobbling around with great difficulty leaning on a walking stick. I was drawn to ask them what the matter was.

The women told me that the son of the family had drowned right before their eyes. The old man still hadn't lost hope and was asking around if anyone had seen his son.

Their condition was heart-rending and extremely pitiful. On seeing him, I was forced to think why we were so traumatised over the loss of a minor portion of our belongings?

Our house, property, kids and every other thing was absolutely safe in Delhi. If we got lucky enough to escape death and reach home, there would be no need to worry about anything anymore. But what would happen to these people whose future had become uncertain.

We had seen much destruction, but as soon as we were a little safe, we had gone back to talking about things we had left behind in our rooms.

I thought about my black shawl, the new chiffon orange suit, Spyker jeans, my new pair of Reebok shoes and about Parth's goods and gadgets, which he had purchased recently. Everything was new –– jeans, tees, shoes, Digi-Cam, iPod etc. The same was true for Anju as well. Both of us regretted our latest purchases––shawls and expensive stoles that we had picked from Srinagar only the day before. Neha also mourned the loss of her beautiful suits and purses she had purchased.

What had happened to us?

Only a few hours back, stuck in a building fast filling up with water, we had been praying to God to spare our lives. When he had done what we had begged him to do by bringing us to the safe building, we began demanding that he save our material possessions.

What about these locals, I thought. Around 200 of them had taken shelter in that building. They had lost everything they owned and every worldly pleasure had been snatched away from them, yet they created no nuisance unlike the tourists. Most just sat mum due to the sudden loss of all they owned. For some, who had lost their dear ones, the pain was even worse than that.

I must admit that till then our kids, though scared, had been taking the whole thing like a risky but adventurous expedition. After coming face to face with people who had lost everything they ever possessed, they understood the true extent of the devastation.

I felt like crying at the tragedy that had struck the locals. But I couldn't. Looking at that family, I stood still like a lifeless stalk.

I felt the numbness of those people who could not let even tears roll down and had to just submit to fate and accept this terrible calamity.

How in a night their kingly state
Changed into a beggarly state!
Strange are the ways of life and fate!

It must have taken them many years of toil to accumulate all that they had for their loved ones.

Every young man, in general, starts his career setting high standards for the lifestyle he wants. He tries to remain firm in order to achieve that standard with unwavering will and skill. In the beginning, he moves with great zeal to fulfil his lofty ambitions but gradually, with age catching up, he treads with weary feet to reach his goals. Even then, he leaves no stone unturned to earn more.

But what if his whole setup is shattered in a matter of minutes? How then does he muster courage to start the journey all the way from the beginning?

Such had been the decree of fate of the Kashmiris at that time.

The fruits of their hard work and the sweat of their brow had been consumed by the flood. Within hours they fell prey to an uncertain destiny and none knew what to do. But it was certain they would have to start their lives afresh without a single penny.

This was the picture of a very small part of Kashmir that we were seeing. What about the rest of the valley?

We didn't know anything about it, but some locals said that the flood had hit the entire valley and nothing but water lay all across. They were not aware of the whereabouts of their relatives –– how were they all coping? Were they even alive? Would they be able to see them again? Nothing was certain.

A woman told us that only two days ago, her daughter had been admitted to a hospital for surgery. She had her uterus removed but the operation ran into complications and the daughter had not been conscious till the previous night. Her daughter had a four-year-old son. She didn't know how and where they would be or whether the army had reached the hospital to rescue them.

That woman had stopped crying…how much can someone cry?

There was no end to such woeful tales. The locals were many, many times braver than us. The first thing on all their minds was that if they escaped alive, they would start searching for their lost relatives…they were cautiously optimistic of finding them alive.

We had crossed the first hurdle in this game of saving our lives.

Now it could be declared that…
Even if we have to strive,
At least we would be alive!

We had come out of the danger zone and were sure that we wouldn't drown as there was two more floors in the building to climb up to in case water rose again.

Little did we realize in those grateful moments that this was just the trailer of a horror film. The full movie was yet to be seen.

The hotel management had allotted one room to us as we were their guests. The room was quite comfortable and fully furnished, but there was nothing to eat or drink.

The first and half of the second floor of this building were lost beneath standing water. Outside the building, all we could see was an expanse of muddy water 13-14 feet high. But there wasn't a single drop of water that could moisten our lips.

We looked at the scowling heavens, the only source of clean drinking water. But how could we pray for even a single drop of rain after the havoc it had wrecked?

We felt trapped between two monsters, the storm in the building and the storm in the water. We watched closely the steadily swelling levels outside and struggled against the oppressive press of people inside.

Our men lay on the dirty, cold floor and women shrivelled small to fit on the bed. We couldn't do anything about either. Many people could be seen wandering in every part of the hotel—corridors, rooms, staircases—seemingly aimlessly, but eagle-eyed to find anything edible.

While the sea of water lashed the hotel from outside, inside people grappled with a tide of anxiety, fear and hunger.

Some were engaged in struggles over petty issues — bickering over a place to sit or resolving arguments among children.

I saw two men abusing each other. Their kids had been trying to wrestle a cap out of each other's grips. One of them had found it somewhere and both claimed to be the rightful owners. Their fathers, instead of disciplining them, had jumped into the fray, taken their respective kids' sides and the matter had escalated unnecessarily.

In fact, this was the scene everywhere. No one knew any peace of mind. The whole throng was perplexed and was spending time in illusions and delusions.

All were like landed on an island surrounded by water on all sides. The difference was, that instead of mesmerising and picturesque beauty, we were facing a terrifying tableau.

In my opinion, the situation on an island might have been much better. We would at least have something to eat like wild fruits, or could drink coconut water. We could signal passing aircraft to get some help and could make a fire at night to protect us from the chill. We might have had certain choices there. But here we were utterly powerless.

We were confined among solid, material things like chairs, tables, ropes, clothes, utensils and building materials sans a drop of liquid to soothe our parched throats. And if we did not find something to eat soon, we would take to eating anything that came our way.

Currently, all we could hear was bawling children and fathers yelling at them to go back to their moms. And all we could see was everyone sitting idle, with time hanging heavy on their hands. All terrified and tense, struggling to accept that they might have to spend the chilly night in this hell.

One hour followed another. We were condemned to endless waiting as no one could do anything. No one had the faintest idea what could be done.

We did not know what we were waiting for. Was it for a miracle we waited? Or a supernatural being to come and rescue us from this quagmire?

It is an undeniable fact that throughout our lives we wait for one thing or another—an event, a person, examination results, an interview, a call, a better lover, a marriage proposal, the right time or for death even.

Sometimes, we are not even sure whether we are waiting at the right place, the right time, the right day, for the right person or for right thing. Still we wait, whether we admit it or not.

I am not sure about others, but I have always waited with a faint hope that something surely will happen to relieve me from all mental and physical agonies I have undergone in the past decade. A day will certainly come when my kids will grow up, their fortunes brighten and success smile upon them. Our wretched state would turn into a blessed state.

Yet, this wait for happy days seems interminable.

The very same thing was happening to us at CH2.

We had no watches, no phones, no schedules, no direction, no clue and most importantly no source of information about how long this ordeal would last. For how long we would have to wallow in this whirlpool of anxiety, insecurity and darkness?

So the ritual of anticipating and waiting continued.

Suddenly, we got a glimpse of a boat passing by. It was jam-packed with old people, young women and some infants. Army men were carrying the babies cautiously in their arms, treating them very gently and handling them with extreme care. Almost all passengers in the boat had painful and drained expressions.

We teared up on seeing that boat and the passengers, and a frisson of hope ran through the entire building. The way forward suddenly became clear and we realised only a boat could rescue us from this cage of water we were imprisoned in. Our hopes suddenly took flight from the swamp of uncertainty and cluelessness.

Though optimism returned, we had no idea when the army men would show up for us.

After that first boat disappeared out of sight, it was decided that everybody would thump on the thick window panes of their rooms so that our presence on the fourth floor of the building could be noticed by the passing boats. Otherwise, they would just whiz past and we would be left hopeless and hapless again.

How we wished there was a balcony or roof to hail the boats from!

But even this plan of attracting attention wasn't easy at all because no boat was to be seen on that vast ocean after the one that energised us all. Many hours later, one or two did reappear but they didn't come anywhere close to our hotel. We were not the ones they were interested in.

But hope is a strange beast. The crowd still believed the army would come for us too eventually and they pinned all their hopes on the boats' return.

Our room was on the fourth floor and whenever we spotted a boat from the window, we would rush down to the second floor since they were accessible only from that level.

But the second floor had morphed into a freezing tunnel of filthy water up to 4 feet high. To add to our misery, power cut had turned the entire building into a dark maze of corridors and staircases. We had to blindly guess our way to move towards the intended destination.

Anyone aiming for that one opening on the second floor had to navigate this terrifying, flooded cavern even if it made them wet through and through. In addition to the darkness and waist-high water, there was the crowd to deal with. The corridors and staircases were packed with people, almost 70-80 of them struggling to navigate it at all times.

Unlike in the previous building, there were no plans here of an organized evacuation. Earlier, there was a clear goal—reach the next building, and it was clear that everyone would get a chance to cross. Hence, a plan could be put in place. Here, no one knew if anyone would come to rescue us. We had been able to spot the rescuers only because the hotel lay en route to a hospital that they were evacuating. There was no guarantee that we were going to be rescued at all.

What added to the mess was the fact that people were increasingly becoming desperate due to hunger, cold and fatigue. More people were packed here than the other building, with no discipline or organization whatsoever.

It was each man to himself.

Everybody had one target—that one room on the second floor whose window had been smashed so people could step out into a boat if it came by.

The entrance to that room was choked. Everybody wanted to get in and nobody gave way to others. They ferociously guarded their spots and went up in arms against anyone who tried to push in. People weren't wrong in doing so since it was a matter of life and death.

But because there was no guarantee of being rescued, and freezing water covered the floor, people could not wait there permanently. They would wander back to the floors above for some warmth and rest. So sometimes, one could wriggle ones way to the room.

When people did manage to reach the room and wade through it, they had to sit on the 'platform.' The team that had earlier helped us reach the building, had used a bed, tables, chairs and broken wooden pieces and joined them altogether to form a platform along the window.

Since the water was about 4 feet high, people would climb up on the platform and sit there hoping to catch a boat's attention. Only 7-8 people could be accommodated at a time because the platform could break if overloaded sending all on it into the water. If by chance a boat stopped, people would step in it from the platform very cautiously. If they weren't careful, a fall in the swirling water was guaranteed.

But whether the boat would take anyone along or not was God's will.

The whole process of reaching the platform took tremendous effort and time coupled with a lot of luck. And when a boat passed by without taking any notice, people would have to wait there again in wet clothes shivering in the cold water to try and catch attention of the next passing boat.

Provided a boat came.

People couldn't leave the spot they had reached after so much trouble. But for how long could one sit in a freezing room in wet clothes? Tired and shivering, they would eventually relinquish their post. Others standing around would rush to take their place.

Half dead, people would slosh their way back to the fourth floor via the bone-chillingly cold and crowded icebox of a corridor.

One thing was very astonishing –– all local Kashmiris seemed able to handle this disaster with patience and were constantly able to figure a way out of precarious situations. Like this platform they had constructed. They were actively trying to find ways to survive the catastrophe.

Unlike the guests, who seemed totally focussed on making the situation worse by exaggerating every discomfort and problem that presented itself.

We sat like nawabs expecting the staff to do everything needful because we had paid for the rooms! We forgot that if something went wrong, all would die the same death. I don't think apart from a few names mentioned earlier, any other guests were ready to do anything.

After a few hours of waiting, the hope of a boat coming by to pick anyone at CH2 came under a huge cloud. But the crowd couldn't stop shouting aloud and scampering towards the room at every single sighting.

Our group also ran to the second floor many, many times that day. We were deadbeat and felt that our last hours were near at hand. Still we had to gather courage, energy and strength to repeat the same process whenever we heard the word BOAT.

Every single time we grit our teeth and pushed through the frosty hallway to the window of hope, wishing that this would be the last journey out of this nightmare.

Our clothes were wet, cold, clingy and muddy. In addition, the skin under the clothes was coated in a layer of sticky mud and it was getting itchy all over. We got terrible rashes under the arms and legs, which made movement difficult.

But nobody complained. Saving life was the top priority.

At around 1:30 a.m.

After repeating the journey so many times that we lost count, we came back to our room completely drained and flopped onto the bed in wet clothes. The cold that night can hardly be described.

Each one of us was engaged in a personal combat ——

with freezing temperature
with wet clothes
with hunger
with fatigue
with fear.

Nobody spoke to anyone. All were fast losing hope of being saved.

I was lying at the extreme corner of the bed, farthest away from the door. Parth, even during those desperate hours, was very anxious about my comfort and was doing whatever best he could with the limited resources at his disposal.

We had not even settled down properly when we heard another shout.

BOAT!

CHAPTER 5

8th September 2014

Around 2 a.m.

*"*Boat aa gayi!*"*[50] somebody shouted.

The scream *"JALDI CHALO! JALDI KARO!"*[51] shook every single bone in our bodies. All rose to a man and bolted in the direction of the voice. Even though the crowd was sapped of all energy, no one ignored the command and just pushed through with all their might.

It's difficult to imagine just how much effort was required to reach our destination. We were jumping over other people including our own group members to get ahead –– half-running, half-falling, and at times even crawling to reach that room.

Not a ray of light penetrated the corridors to tell us whether we were going in the right direction. We just followed the sound of frantic footsteps and the noise of people running.

---

[50] *Boat has arrived*
[51] *Hurry Up!*

No one worried, bothered or cared about anyone else. No emotional concern could be spared for others.

It felt like we had drunk copious quantities of wine and under its influence we lurched ahead intoxicated. As if some enchanter had cast a magical spell on us and we mindlessly obeyed him.

How much the fear of death can terrorise, we experienced that day.

We didn't even bother to check whether our family members were with us or not. All were in a mad rush to get ahead of others in this race to survive. Getting hands on the boat was the sole motto.

Even the icy corridor that needed to be crossed first didn't give us pause or weaken our resolve. The primal urge to stay alive had kicked in and we ran forward, even with paralysed legs and numb hearts.

Though I was moving with every ounce of energy I could muster, I lagged behind as I was the last to come out of the room. People who were near the door went first. Others at the back had to wait for their turn. Nobody cared whether their companions were with them or not.

As we moved forward, people from other rooms joined the herd. It was beyond chaotic.

Packed in the crowd, I reached the end of the corridor on the fourth floor and suddenly realised I had forgotten my spectacles in the room. While sleeping, I had kept them on a stool. On hearing the word BOAT, I had bolted upright and rushed to the door to get out. In that confused state of mind, I had forgotten to pick my glasses.

Sans spectacles, I was as good as blind. Almost by reflex and without a second thought, I turned back in the direction of our room. People tried to push me down and walk all over me since I was moving in the direction opposite to that of the manic crowd. I simply became another obstacle they had to knock down in their dash towards the boat.

Somebody shouted at me, *"Pagal ho gayi hai kya"? Ulti taraf kyo bhaag rahi hai?"*[52]

But I had no time to reply other than focussing on my focus!

It was a long and dark way back that I traversed with a terrorised spirit. Panting heavily, I somehow reached the room and quickly grabbed my glasses. As soon as I wore them, I felt a little steadier and regained a sense of clarity.

And now I had to run back the same way. Whenever I recall those moments, the blood in my veins freezes.

On my way back, I suddenly realised all rooms had become empty and I was alone in the corridor on the fourth floor. The dark and deserted place immediately turned ghostly. I felt I was trapped in a witch's web and she was forcing me run from this end to that.

---

[52] *Have you gone mad? Why are you running in the wrong direction?*

Frightening thoughts gripped my mind. I wanted to scream but my voice died in my throat and no words came out. I felt as though all my companions had left me in a lurch and abandoned me to save their own lives. I was terror-stricken and wondered if I would be able to live through this dangerous mission of retrieving a pair of spectacles. My entire body and mind was caught in the grip of catastrophic thoughts.

All it took was a few minutes in which I went back to the room and then rushed wildly back to reach my mates. But those minutes seemed like an eternity. I was running as if I was in a marathon and I was the sole participant left behind. I had to go across the finishing line by hook or by crook because survival was at stake and death the price of losing.

It was the faint, greyish moonlight in the pitch-dark sky outside that faintly guided my way. From all sides I heard haunting sounds in the eerie abandoned floor…. ssshhhhhhh, hissssss, braapppp… I shivered and my head swam.

It looked as if a ghost or a giant gorilla was chasing me and if I didn't hurry, he would catch hold of me and suck the very last drop of my blood. I was too petrified to even look back and kept pushing ahead. The devil of fear inside me prodded me to move faster. In my panic, I kept tripping and falling but after straining every nerve, every muscle, I reached the end of the corridor.

From there, falling, crawling I went down the staircase to the second floor. Those frightening hissing and groaning sounds were still following me but something had fired me up and even in that rattled condition I emerged from the mouth of that deathly den alive.

But I couldn't dare to look back to check who was chasing me. As quickly as I could, I pushed myself into the safety of the crowd.

Moving ahead, I tried to locate my people but the crowd was thick and no one from my group was standing there. Once again, my heart sank and I felt as if I had been abandoned and left absolutely alone.

Nobody was ready to give me the slightest room to enter the corridor of the second floor.

I was wailing and begging people, "Please let me get in. My family is standing at the other end and I have lagged behind." But nobody relented.

Some even ignored my plea and one big bully of a guy said, "Madam, everyone has to leave, you are not the exception. When your turn comes, you will be allowed to go. Now don't create a scene here, just wait for your turn."

I had to surrender, as I was unable to revolt and push through. But I relaxed a bit because at least I was among people, safe from the devil haunting the empty corridors above.

The place was a mess and it was stinking. It was already overcrowded and packed, and yet people were trying to thrust themselves into any gap they thought they could slip into. Everyone was struggling to withstand the force of gushing water despite being drained of all energy and strength.

Suddenly, I saw Parth looking back through the mob and our eyes met. We both shouted frantically to each other. I started crying and a man standing beside me took pity. He said to the others, "Let her go to her son. See that boy there. He is crying for his mother."

He helped me pass through that jam-packed corridor. Bit by bit, I reached where my group was and hugged Parth tight.

Nobody bothered to ask why I had been left behind. Only Parth said, "Where did you disappear? I was looking for you but people did not let me go back to find you." He gripped my hand and said, "Now you be with me and don't go off anywhere on your own."

I didn't say anything, just obeyed. The truth is that there was nothing to say. It was a time of great stress and people were preparing themselves for the worse.

All women were made stand in the front row so that they could be sent in the army boats first. We were shivering more than it was humanly possible, but didn't dare to move an inch. Every passing moment froze us some more. Our feet became numb and our teeth started chattering and we had almost turned into statues.

At 3 a.m.

Finally a boat came. Immediately, pushing, pulling and heaving started all over again.

Though many women were sitting at the edge of the platform, the boatmen didn't let any of them step into the boat. They had come to rescue specific people — the Chief Manager of a bank and his wife. The couple was old and was stranded with us.

There was another group of eight to ten people who had come to Kashmir to play golf. On seeing the boat, they wanted to send their golf kits in the boat. They tried their best to persuade the boatmen to allow them to send the kits as they were very expensive. But the boatmen explained to them that they had come to rescue the old couple only and they could not take anybody else. The boatmen were firm. They asked others to hold on until they returned.

The rescuers didn't want to burden the boat as it was not too big or spacious and they didn't want to take any risk by overloading as it was late at night. In addition, they had been assigned the job of rescuing that old couple and drop them to the army camp safely.

None in the crowd knew about the presence of the banker except Mr. Mehra who had met us in the previous building.

Since this ordeal had begun, Mr Mehra had been visiting all rooms one by one. He was constantly talking to people trying to figure some way out of this calamity. He was a very witty and active man who was proactive at all times. Unlike others who were sitting around wringing hands but doing nothing. They had thrown themselves at the mercy of the Lord.

A third of the crowd comprised of women trying their best to manage their kids who, with every tick of the clock, were getting crankier. Of the remaining two thirds, i.e. men, some were old and sick. So only a few could have engaged in some useful activity to deal with the situation. But most of them did not show any eagerness to do anything at all. They had just accepted that their end was near and were just sitting around with no faith in their fate.

A man who doesn't trust himself
Can never truly trust anyone else.

We didn't know what Mr. Mehra did, but he managed to send his wife in the boat with the banker couple! His relentless efforts proved fruitful.

We were also determined to get into the boat by any means, so were pushing others out of the way. But the army men pushed us back assuring us at the same time that they would be back after dropping the chief and his wife safely at the camp.

Though their words belied a lack of conviction, the crowd was left with no other option but to go by their words and prepare for another round of waiting.

Finally, the boat set off with the chief, his wife and Mrs. Mehra. The rest settled into waiting, envying the rescued group.

Those were perilous moments. Nobody moved an inch. We stood like stones in the dirty and stinking water.

The stones might wish that someday they would be placed on dry, clean land where they might breathe fresh air. We were in the exact situation and hoped someone would rescue us from this cold, suffocating cavern.

We clenched our teeth and forced ourselves to stay motionless in the frozen water motivated by a flickering hope that the boat might return that night to save us and transport us to a place with sunshine.

But no one came.

The prospects of a boat's arrival were getting thinner with each wink, yet we stood in the glaciated water for at least another hour. There descended a silence so thick, you could cut it with a knife.

When it sank into us that the rescuers wouldn't be back, we embarked on the same tedious journey to our room with heavy heart and steps. In a devastated state, we entered our room and fell on the beds like dead carcass. Some of us stretched on the cold floor.

No hunger
No thirst
No sentiments
No natural calls…

We lay like lumps of dead lamb without any traces of living human beings left in us…all religiously meditating upon the word BOAT and waiting for it with bated breath.

It had been a taxing and frustrating day. After every few minutes tears welled up in our eyes making us more and more despondent.

Around 4 a.m.

The remaining hours passed tossing and shivering.

We were tired to our last bones and horribly hungry.

Surprisingly, we still managed to doze off.

In the morning when I entered the washroom, it was stinking as many people had already used it and there was not a single drop of water to clean it. I tried the washroom of the nearby room but found the same foul smell hanging heavy there as well.

A waiter passing by said, "Ma'am, all washrooms of the hotel are stinking. Better use yours only."

I came back to my room and mustered courage to enter the hellhole. I held my breath while urinating but still couldn't keep myself from inhaling the stench. I vomited out whatever little was left in my empty stomach.

I rushed to the corridor as soon as I had relieved myself. There, I greedily inhaled lungsful of 'fresh' air.

We were out of electricity, water, food, means of communication and every other essential thing. We were trapped in a dungeon just waiting to see what would happen next.

Time ticked by in a slow, silent crawl. We resumed the task of staring out through the sound proof glasses of the windows, thump on them nevertheless and shout for help.

Hours kept passing in slow motion, whittling down our hopes with despair and dejection.

At 10 a.m.

Every one in the building wandered around this temporary shelter trying to kill time. It seemed as if people from all around the National Highway had gathered in CH2 and was on a hunt for anything to eat.

This hotel had been inaugurated only one-and-a-half months back. It was a beautiful place, nicely designed and tastefully furnished. The rooms, the beds, the blankets and the bathrooms, all were very new. When we had checked in, the place was gleaming and bathed in fresh fragrances.

But now it had been converted into a public place whose every belonging had been looted. The hungry mob had robbed all cans, chocolates, fruits and other items from the small refrigerators in the rooms. Not a single drop of water was left even in the ice-trays.

I peeped into the next room and saw two small kids, perhaps siblings, fighting over an empty wrapper of a biscuit packet. One was licking the crumbs from it and the other was trying to snatch it from him. Both were fighting over it like wild animals.

In the corridor, I happened to set my eyes on a strange, sad sight. An old woman in her late seventies had found a small, stale and dirty piece of bread. I don't know whether deliberately or not, but I felt she was trying her best to hide it from prying eyes so that she could eat it all by herself.

Covertly, she slid the piece in her pocket. My eyes kept following her and I found her standing in a remote corner swallowing that small piece as quickly as she could manage.

Hunger can push people to any point!

Everyone scavenged for something to eat. Some people found pieces of noodles and opted to chew on them raw so that they could keep themselves going somehow.

What an unimaginably horrifying situation…!

When I passed by the kitchen, I saw not a single grain of rice or sugar left in any corner or in the utensils. I spotted a boy eating salt from a sachet and another tearing apart an empty packet of tomato sauce to lick it.

The entire building had been thoroughly ransacked in the hunt for food. Nothing could be found anywhere.

I walked towards the staircase, sat down on the dirty steps and gazed dismally at the whole scene. Hunger was running rampant.

How to find even a tiny morsel became the sole aim for every starving soul.

Abruptly, memories of how, once before, abundance had turned into scarcity flashed before me.

Sitting on the steps, frames from the past when I had to dig deep to fetch food for my kids ran like a reel of a film before my eyes.

We had seen the brighter side of life when Anil used to sing on big stages making the gatherings sway with spiritual fervour.

He and I were such a proud and happy couple! But our togetherness lasted only a short time and then his hand was snatched away from mine, never to be clasped again.

I had to experience the darker side of life then.

Everyone worships the rising Sun, and the Sun of my life had set, never to rise again!

Money lends power to words.
Sans money, there stayed no sun in my sermons.

As long as we had wealth, people listened to us. Anil was loved and so was I. People valued not only his words, but mine too. But when he departed and our wealth vanished, my words lost their power they had over people. Sans a husband, my words lost all charm.

We became an unwanted, unappreciated lot. Nobody visited us as we might ask for help. I couldn't even spare time to weep for the departed soul as thousands of problems lay before me which were only mine to sort.

A one-time fiery woman, I was transformed into a timid and inarticulate person.

I was left to raise my kids the way I chose, but which way to choose I did not know!

In those days, after putting my kids to sleep, I would hold Krishna's idol tightly in my hands, cry and ask him, "Will you be with us or leave us like the others have? My husband worshipped you and sang your *bhajans* his entire life and see what you did to him? You took him away in his prime, at the zenith of his career. How could you do so, and why? Now, how do I bring up my kids? Whom should I turn to?

It's your duty to rear my kids as Anil always asked me to have undeterred faith in you and I did have and I do have.

O Lord! Kindly guide me through this critical time. Kindly, kindly row us to the shore this one last time."

And numberless nights passed this way. By dawn, I would feel as if I had become more competent to face the responsibilities of the day.

Everyday, I encountered loads of unpleasant experiences. Each moment I had to worry about the bills——telephone, electricity, car fuel, school fee, kitchen supplies, the dues of housing society, and hundreds of other expenses. To meet these, I worked ceaselessly.

I had to sweat blood to earn my bread.

Despite working non-stop all day, I never enjoyed an hour of peaceful sleep. Actually, sleep also departs with the departed soul. That man takes away your essence and emotions with him and leaves flesh and bones only in a hollow, living mask.

The world was packed with people but my eyes would scan streets for my lost soul mate, but to no avail. Every bhajan singer seemed to be him but when he turned around, it was always a stranger.

I would drive my car to look for forlorn places to weep aloud for hours as I didn't want to depress my kids more by crying in front of them.

Weeping I would ask Kanhaiya——
Wither is fled that visionary gleam?
Wither is that glory and dream?
Why did the glow of our partnership dim?

Every second of my life, I asked God the same thing again and again and again. The only answer I got was, "My dear child, he who has disappeared from this world can never re-appear. You haven't lost everything. Those who are with you are equally precious. So be theirs with all heart. I'm there to assist you."

You just start making the web.
I'll provide you the thread.

And I started my own event management company called EVENTUA.

It was a totally new world for me and I had no idea how to run a business. But I had made a few friends who were in the same profession and I kept moving ahead with their inputs. Dawn to dusk, I would go from one office to the next to pitch to clients and convince them to give me a chance.

But people did not trust me. Everyone's words differed but all answered 'NO'. This long string of failures did not affect my confidence. I knew all I needed was just one break, one chance, one beat to bang.

My relentless visits to companies bore fruit eventually. I got a few opportunities and succeeded in managing a few small events and shows and by the end of the year 2003, I had organised some bigger events outstandingly. My hard work, honesty and straight dealings attracted more and bigger clients.

I remember doing road shows for Honda Eterno, LML, Scorpio and other automobile companies; Skoda Superb Car launch in Delhi Golf Club with the German ambassador and many famous personalities in attendance; a fashion show for JD Institute of Fashion technology; Artists Live in water parks and Tivoli Garden; theme nights in 5-stars properties like The Taj, Bristol Hotel and discotheques; and Star Night in Talkatora Stadium sponsored by Rana Sariya and others.

Life had taken a smooth turn and I was busy day and night nursing my fledging company.

Suddenly an incident turned the track of our train in a completely different direction.

One day, when I returned home from the work, I found Parth severely injured on the head. Kashish had taken him to the nursing home and got him stitched up and bandaged but had no money to clear the bill.

Actually, he never had any. I still couldn't spare anything because running the business and paying off all the debts and bills took first priority.

Kashish was sitting beside Parth and crying. Neither said or asked anything of me but their eyes narrated their pain. That day, I realised I had prioritised my grief and my challenges over their sorrow, which was no less devastating. After all, at such a tender age they had lost their father and yet had never made me feel their loneliness and sense of loss.

In my own aggrieved mental state, I had been neglecting my kids and running around to get more cash to buy comforts for them. But at what cost?

My dear kids had lost their father and their mother at one go as she was never accessible to love, guard or guide them. Both the kids, in a short span of time, had matured much more than me. They never cried in front of me, never made any undue demands and had accepted their penury without any query.

That was the deciding day
No stepping out for the sake of pay.

I embraced both of them tightly and we dissolved into tears. Then and there I promised them, "Whatever the future holds, we will all be together and I will not go out to make money. If God is really kind, He will send us a source of income at home only. I won't leave my kids alone to suffer anymore."

I kept my word and shut EVENTUA when we needed money the most and quickly spiralled down another whirlpool of struggle for existence.

At that crucial time, Anil's words––Leave everything to God, he will never let us down–– echoed in my ears and gave me courage to start afresh from home. But God doesn't grant his grace easily. He tests one's tolerance and when he is satisfied, he pours out his gifts exuberantly on him.

He did the same with us.

When all means of earning were closed to me, He guided me to the path of imparting education. I started a coaching institute 'Triumph Academy' at my place.

It was not easy to get students as nobody was ready to believe that a simple lady would be able to teach their kids well. In fact, I have to admit, I myself was not quite sure whether I would be able to teach students with confidence.

One day, in the temple of our apartments, I met my friend Rita Jain and asked her to send her kids for grammar classes. She was the first to vest her faith in me and sent Shreya and Shashwat, her kids. They were my first students.

God bless the family!

I started teaching primary class students during the day. At night I prepared myself to teach higher classes. I kept the fees to a bare minimum so that students could afford it. Hence, even after much toil, I was unable to meet all expenditures. I was unable to pay my children's school fee on time as I was always short of funds.

Then a dear friend came up with a suggestion, "Why don't you get your children admitted to a government school instead of sending them to a public school? The fee is comparatively low there and it will give you a hassle-free life and you won't have to work so much."

But I didn't take her advice as I knew the quality of education in an English medium school would equip them with better skills and make them self-reliant in today's competitive world.

I myself belonged to a very normal family and my father had always laid stress on educating his kids even with limited resources. He always told me, "Renu, study as much as you can as education will be of great use to you in times to come. If you utilise this time wisely, you'll be able to earn more degrees which will be priceless for you."

And I had tried to follow his words.

I completed my graduation and post graduation from Delhi University in 1987 and continued acquiring more knowledge. My father's sermon was proving it's worth now making me earn for my family using that education.

How could I settle for anything less for my children whose lives had just started and there was a long way for them to tread? I was determined to educate them on my own terms and never short-change the quality. They continued going to Public Schools.

To nurture students who came to me, I invested everything I had. Kashish and Parth also stood by me and contributed whatever and however they could. Our goal to survive guided us well and kept us pressing on despite several challenges.

When my students showed exceptional results, heaps of new students started approaching us, giving new wings to our goal of stepping out of the vicious clutches of poverty.

When a student of mine topped in 12th standard in English and got admission in English Honours at Delhi University, her parents came to my place and said, "Renu Ma'am, you have to teach her further because we got her admitted in the English course only because we have faith in you."

I didn't know what to say! But I agreed. And with this I started another coaching centre for higher studies called 'Renu Mittal Concepts'.

After that, my daily route was from Paschim Vihar to Nayi Sarak, the biggest market of books in Delhi. Every now and then I would be found there sitting on the floor of the bookshops and finding out about authors, novels, help books etc. I would come back loaded with sacks full of books. I would spend whole nights and days reading, writing, making notes for all three years of the English Honours course.

But the quest for knowledge took hold of me and I started preparing for IELTS, TOEFL, PTE and other competitive exams. I also enrolled in an English Honours course myself and completed it.

By God's grace, I succeeded in every effort I made and we survived and thrived. Year by year, our condition and confidence started improving.

Now suddenly in 2014, what had gone wrong and why had our destiny brought us to Kashmir to this calamity?

Around 3 p.m.

We were experiencing two menacing moods of nature — flood outside the building and famine inside. Both were equally diabolic and demonic, ready to crush us with all their force.

With every moment, problems worsened. More hunger, more thirst, more cold, more suffocation, more agitation, more violence.

Some locals were trying to arrange for a boat. They knew a man living a few houses away had one. Everyone gave suggestions and ideas on how to tow it to the hotel...some good, some bad, some silly. But all that back and forth went in vain as arranging for a boat while being trapped inside a concrete building was absolutely impossible.

The discussions over this scheme took up a large amount of time. It was almost nightfall and they were still at it –arguing, quarrelling, mocking, abusing and in a few instances physically hitting too as everyone wanted to send their families first when the boat arrived.

It was almost comical because there was no boat available and yet people fought with passion over who would go first. Finally, after much debate, it was decided that if a boat came, whether from the neighbourhood or the army boat, the women and kids would be sent first and men would follow later.

But at every sighting of a boat, the 'settled' matter would heat up as nobody was ready to be separated from their family members. Whenever a boat was sighted, the place turned into an inferno of heaving and screaming agitated human bodies. In wet clothes that refused to dry and sticky mud clinging to skins, wailings for the boats continued.

We sat silently in our room, watching the wrathful water engulfing whatever lay in its way.

Everywhere broken branches from collapsed trees were hanging at crazy angles. Only the upper parts of the lofty trees, say 10-12 inches, were visible. The rest were totally submerged in water. The canopies seemed to have joined their heads together and they looked like green clouds floating on muddy water.

The whole area looked like a messy mural, painted by a artist in a drunken and dizzy state.

I was reminded of the famous French painter Jean Dubuffet who coined the concept of 'Art Brut' or 'Raw Art' in 1940s. Such art is made by people who haven't received any formal training, but who, through sheer talent and artistic insight, produce wonders using waste materials. Just like Nek Chand has created the Rock Garden in Chandigarh.

On looking at the scene outside the window, I began to think that a desire to create a miraculous and massive mosaic with broken pieces must have arisen in the heart of the Almighty.

To carry out his plan, he required beautiful raw materials. Since Kashmir is incomparable in its marvelousness, he perhaps zeroed in on the mesmerising valley.

Then, to gather the scrap, he hit the valley with strong strokes of His powerful hammer and then there lay uncountable bits of trees, timber and tins in every corner. Now the piles of raw material were available in abundance. The Lord could create as many murals as His heart desired with those pieces.

Perhaps the beauty of the valley became its nemesis and brought it to this dishevelled state, trapping us here in this calamity.

The game of Gods lay heavy on the valley!
And we were to pay the price with our lives!

CHAPTER 6

Sitting in CH2 waiting for the boat, I recalled how I was in a different world only a few days ago.

2nd September 2014

Around 1 p.m.

After spending a splendid time in Nishat, our group of nine journeyed further to Chashme Shahi, famous for its natural spring of mineral water. The taste of water was so pure, and divine, far away from all impurities of urban life.

A Kashmiri man told us, "Our first Prime Minister, Pandit Jawahar Lal Nehru, was very fond of this water. According to him, no water on Earth was as pure as this at Chashme Shahi."

We were amused at his words but when we had a few sips, we felt his sentiments were absolutely true. We filled our bellies and two bottles to quench our thirst later on.

Then we headed to Dal Lake as fast as we could. We didn't want to let even an hour go by without enjoying the treasures of the valley.

The daintiness of the lake hypnotised our eyes and bound them to its bounties. The small floating world left the whole group amazed.

Kashmiris have created a floating paradise with all necessities and luxuries on the waters of the Dal. There are markets, chemists, homes, cafes, butcher shops, grocery outlets, fair-price shops, handicrafts and carpets showrooms — all on the gently lapping waters of the Dal.

We hired two *shikaras* and enjoyed magnificent royal rides in them. The *shikara* boatmen took us to a showroom of beautiful handicrafts items, but the bargain didn't work out and we came back empty handed.

We enjoyed a fabulous time floating on the lake. We ate fruit salad and *bhuttas*[53], and drank *kahwa*[54] listening to and enjoying the banter among the teens. Then followed the inevitable but wonderful photo session.

The whole day just flew by.

At dusk, when we returned to the lake, a fascinating spectacle lay before our eyes. There stood many rows of splendid houseboats, the 'Gurkha' of Welcome Group.

We were taken aback at the artistry on display! The boats looked like small palaces from the Mughal Era. The tops of the boats were carved in ravishing red with beautiful

---

[53]   *roasted corn on cob*

[54]   *Kashmiri tea*

designs etched on the sides. Inside were tables, chairs, carpets, utensils and gorgeous sceneries on the walls. The highlight was the *nazakat*[55] of the language the attendants spoke with. It made us feel we were in an Emperor's palace.

The captivating line up of these altogether spectacular boats made the Dal even more enchanting.

I began wondering who first explored the idea of creating houses on water. Man's imagination can produce magic anywhere—sky, land or water. His endurance makes him withstand floods, thunderstorms, landslides and earthquakes and enables him to do divine things as he had done in creating houseboats on the Dal.

Our attendant was an old fellow who showed exceptional hospitality. He offered *kahwah* and then served a never-ending list of mouth-watering delicacies, after which he escorted us to our respective rooms.

When Parth opened the doors of our room, we both stood mesmerised at the lavishness of the space. The bed was surrounded with lovely white net curtains on all four sides, making it look like a compact and cozy box.

I slipped into the bed like a princess. Then we both started clicking photos crazily leaving no corner and no angle unexplored. After satiating ourselves with loads of wonderful snaps, we went to the dining hall to try the very artistically served dinner. The aroma of the food stoked our hunger and

---

[55] *elegance*

increased it manifold. We tried every dish and ate every bite with great relish before coming out to the lobby to join other members of our party.

At around 8 p.m.

It was time for Tambola. Anshu was calling out the numbers and Parth kept winning each time. They were sitting in opposite corners of the room, so there was nothing to be suspicious about.

But when Parth won for the third time, it was way too fishy for us to ignore. How come luck was favouring him so much?

Manoj took this seriously and when the next game started, he observed both of them closely.

This is what he found…

When all of us were busy trying to locate numbers on our cards, Parth very cleverly took a snapshot of his card and sent it to Anshu who then called out only those numbers. That was how Parth won each time. But the wicked and smirking Anshu and Parth were finally caught red handed this time! We grabbed all the money from them and gave them a good beating.

Then the party decided to play cards. Again the boys tried to bluff, but their tricks couldn't fool us this time.

Around 9:30 p.m.

We saw a *shikara* rowing towards us. Two local shopkeepers came out with a couple of bundles of shawls and displayed amazing examples of their craftsmanship. We purchased showpieces––wooden boxes, pen stands and others curios–– after a handsome bargain. Then came another boat with a collection of purses and wallets. His collection was undoubtedly pleasing but it left us in dismay because the seller did not lower prices to match our offers. He departed without enriching us with his fabulous collection.

The day had been thrilling but tiring too. Even so, nobody wanted the enthralling experiences to end. But we had to rest, as the following day was packed with as many amazing adventures.

Reluctantly, we retired to our rooms. When Parth and I slipped into our bed, it didn't take us long to slip into a royal, restful slumber.

3rd September 2014

The day broke with pleasing sounds of pitter-patter.

I got up and came out to sit in the lobby to enjoy every beautiful bit of the foggy and chilly morning. I sat at the entrance admiring the enchanting scene. After half an hour, Anju and Sanjay joined me. We soaked up the mesmerising beauty of the rain-drenched morning with joy.

When we were having our tea, a shawl seller appeared and showed us a wonderful range of pashminas. We noted down his mobile number and assured him that on our return from

Gulmarg, we would certainly come to his house to look at the entire collection and may be buy a few.

After the delicious breakfast, we got into a *shikara to go across to the other bank where our Tempo driver was waiting to take us to Gulmarg.

By now, the drizzle had turned into a downpour.

The ride was rough, but the boatman seemed unperturbed. The lashing rain rocked the boat making it wobble and he seemed to be struggling to balance it. With every stroke of his oar, we felt that the boat would turn turtle and we would splash into the lake.

Barely one or two *shikaras could be seen around. They were perhaps going about their regular jobs, but were very far away from us. If something went wrong, they wouldn't be able to come to our rescue.

The boatman assured us that choppy waters were very regular and there was nothing at all to worry.

He reassured us, "Sir, almost every house near Dal has its own small boat just as you people have scooties, bikes, cycles or cars in the cities. Here, the local inhabitants have to row their own small dinghies for the smallest of chores like buying vegetables, medicines, or to go to school."

He pointed at two small kids, who were probably coming back from school, rowing their tiny boat perfectly. To us, it all seemed very frightening. We kept looking at them till they were out of sight.

I asked the boatman, "How are these small kids so brave? From where do they get so much heart?

Are all people living on the lake good swimmers too? Do their kids also know how to swim? Don't parents get petrified when their tiny-tots play wildly on the boats, go to school or for other work rowing their own dinghies?"

He replied, "Ma'am, there is nothing unusual. Our kids have been practicing how to maintain balance in the houseboats since infancy. They will not fall into the water."

Though he answered all my queries, many questions still buzzed around in my mind. If a child by chance looses his balance and falls into water, then how does he save himself? Is he capable of swimming out to safety on his own if nobody is around, or does the water engulf him? Do such incidents happen or have happened here? Or is this horrible scenario only the product of my overactive imagination?

If any such incident does happen, are any doctors, nurses or any other kind of medical assistance accessible at any time round the clock?

In times of emergency, we land inhabitants can rush to any hospital in the vicinity. But what about these water inhabitants? Where and to whom do they rush to? Isn't life here so challenging? Don't they live in constant fear of life every moment?

Doesn't this water scare people at night?

Something very magical must be around to hold them here and compel them to set up their fortune on these wavering tides. Or, is it that they can't find any other corner on Earth to lead their lives?

Is it really worth living on a lake that can turn life threatening any moment and endanger their precious lives?

My mind deliberated on these dilemmas till our boat hit the other shore.

The journey to Gulmarg commenced in the Tempo Traveller in good spirits. We played Ludo, the all time favourite indoor game, and enjoyed it to the fullest. As usual, the older kids troubled and irritated Aarav by hiding his bag––one he always carried packed with all necessary and favourite things like chocolates, pencils, biscuits, games and candies.

We had named it his "survival kit". At that point we couldn't have guessed in our wildest dreams that this bag would live up to its name and how!

It kept raining unceasingly that entire day and we absolutely loved it! On the way, Radhu asked the driver to stop the car as she wished to eat *bhuttas*[56]. All got down and ate not

---

[56]   *roasted corn on cob*

just *bhuttas*[57] but *gol gappe*[58], *bhel puri*[59] and all local street food available.

We saw long rows of apples and walnut orchards. The sight of red apples hanging on the branches of the trees was a very tempting picture.

Hasan, our driver, was a chatterbox and would speak a lot on any given topic. Aarav asked him to pluck a few apples, but he bluntly refused to do so!

He said that Kashmiris have great respect for the peasants and never plunder their produce.

Even after many entreaties and much persuasion, he didn't budge. On the contrary, he began explaining to us that it was reaping time and all the farmers were hopeful of getting a good price for their yield after a yearlong tough grind.

All the trees were loaded with red and ripe apples, and Hasan was sure the owner's jubilation knew no bounds.

He continued telling us that his father was a farmer too and when he was a child, he would help his father in the field.

He made us understand that since the day a farmer starts the entire process of ploughing and sowing to harvest the crop, he undergoes countless sleep-deprived nights fearing

---

[57] *roasted corn on cob*

[58] *street snack*

[59] *street snack*

the uncertainty of the future of the crop. People who haven't gone through the experience can't imagine just how much effort he invests to save it from birds, stray animals, thieves and even envious enemies. When the reaping season arrives, he can't even blink lest his yield be attacked.

What relief he gets on catching a glimpse of the loaded orchard is beyond description! He sheds a thousand tears of happiness, thanking God for letting him accomplish his goal.

After this monologue, Hasan peppered us with questions one after the other, "Sir, do you think a farmer's labour can be priced by any means? Don't you think if I go and pluck apples from his treasure, it would amount to stealing? They are fruits of his mind- and soul-numbing labour. Do we have any right to take their possession without paying for it?"

Sanjay at once replied, "No Hasan, we don't. You are absolutely right. We don't have any right to take even a bite without paying the price for it."

After Hasan's long and moving speech, we felt sorry for making such an unreasonable demand.

Though the matter ended there peacefully, our dear kids felt snubbed and started making faces at him.

Radhika grumbled, "Who does he think he is? What does he think of himself? He lectured us so much on one topic! We just asked for an apple and he read the whole book on a farmer's life."

Anshu growled, "Arrrrgghhhh!! Ask him to hold his tongue else I will break his teeth...I'm just waiting for our journey to be over!"

Parth nodded approvingly and wickedly suggested, "Why to wait till the end of the journey? Let's prank him in Gulmarg. I'll teach him how to yak less."

All grinned gleefully and began hatching a plot to bully.

On the road ahead, we saw stockpiles of picked ripe apples. The rosiness and the satisfaction on the faces of the farmers on seeing the yield was extraordinary. Some were bargaining with buyers and expecting a good price. The following year's prosperity depended on this sale. This was the time to cash in on the hard work they had done day and night.

We were nearing our destination and crossed the flyover that connected Gulmarg and Srinagar. While driving on it, dreaming of soon being in the lap of the legendary beauty of Gulmarg, nobody could have imagined that only within a few hours this flyover would cast its name in the history of Kashmir.

Till that moment, our holidays seemed to have been perfectly planned. The only irritant was the rainfall that refused to take a break. But it did not dampen our enthusiasm one bit.

Since it was pouring steadily, we had started feeling quite cold and hungry. So we decided to fill our bellies first before stepping into the hotel we were staying at.

At 2 p.m.

We stopped at a tiny *dhaba*[60] for lunch. It was a compact space offering a limited range of food on its menu. The owner gave us a warm welcome and immediately got busy in preparing the desired dishes.

To our surprise, he didn't have any helping hand and was running around the place all alone wearing a smile. Within minutes he prepared all the ordered items and served the food cheerfully and we ate to our heart's content.

We noticed Parth and Anshu whispering in Aarav's ear, "Psst…psst.. huss…huss……."

I don't know what the kids were saying, but Aarav went out and said to Hasan,"Driver *bhaiya*[61], I have something for you. Close your eyes and bend down. Only then I'll give it to you."

Hasan said, "First show me what it is."

But Aarav continued insisting on him bending down first. Hasan gave in and closing his eyes, he lowered his head before Aarav.

Aarav smashed a big tomato on his head with all his might and laughed loudly. "I have fooled Hasan *bhaiya!*[62] I have

---

[60] *small roadside eatery*

[61] *brother*

[62] *brother*

124

won! See Anshu *bhaiya*[63] I have done it, now give me your mobile to play games."

Anshu responded angrily,"Aarav! What is this? Don't you have any manners? Is this how you behave with elders?"

Parth and Radhika also joined in. "Aaru! You shouldn't behave this way! Bad boy! Say sorry to Hasan *bhaiya!*[64]

Aarav screeched, "Haawwwww *bhaiya!*[65] This is cheating! You only asked me to do it!"

But the naughty bunch of three exclaimed innocently, "What are you saying Aaru! We never said so! Now you have started telling lies too."

Aaru burst into tears and went to his mother.

Hasan complained to Sanjay and Manoj, "Sir, your kids are way too naughty. Ask them to behave else I won't drive!"

The kids laughed mischievously, "Now Hassan won't lecture us and will drive quietly…"

Sanjay scolded them. "Behave yourselves! Don't be so indecent and disrespectful." He somehow hushed up the matter and asked Hasan to let it go.

---

[63] *brother*

[64] *brother*

[65] *brother*

Hasan had to wash his hair with cold water.

Enraged and shivering to his skin, he drove towards the Khyber Hotel, one of the most spectacularly luxurious five star hotels in Gulmarg.

CHAPTER 7

3rd September 2014

4 p.m.

The grandeur of Khyber hotel! Nature in vibrant hues surrounded the beautiful building.

We had been enduring bitter cold since morning and the lobby provided a cozy haven. Warm relief ran through our veins as soon as we stepped in. The entire place was amazingly done up and we were soon lost in its elegance.

Magnificent and imposing portraits of emperors adorned the walls and they were awe-inspiring. The light, soothing music in the lobby took all of us by surprise. Delicate and exquisite little curious graced the interiors of the hotel.

We looked around the entire place and after admiring every little corner we went into the rooms allotted to us.

Our room itself was fit to be in a palace. It had all the best possible facilities. I drew the curtains aside from the windows, and the scenery outside mesmerised me.

Never ending rows of *Chinar*[66] trees, high mountains, stony passes, small huts and, above all, the music of the raindrops!

"From where has all this water been pouring day and night?" I mused. "Where lies the perennial source of this rain? Oh! Lord Indra, why don't you put brakes on your elephant *Airavata?*[67] Let him rest for a short while."

It seemed as if the Lord had forgotten to turn off a mighty fountain, and that's why it had been raining with such abandon.

Confined to the hotel, we passed the whole day gossiping and goofing around. We rested for some time and then met in the dining hall, had dinner and chatted for a while. Then all wished to catch some sleep so we went back to our rooms.

It was 9 p.m.

I wanted to lie down peacefully but Parth kept on flipping channels on TV making me irritable.

I said, "Turn off the TV and sleep."

"It's 9'o clock Mum and you are asking me to sleep? Is it possible? Do I ever sleep so early?

C'mon! Don't sound so lazy. Let's watch a movie together. I'll make a good cup of tea for you," Parth cajoled.

---

[66] *A deciduous tree*
[67] *Mythological elephant belonging to Lord Indra, God of rain*

I agreed and he settled on the channel showing 'Tum Mile'.

Though I didn't want to postpone my sleep, the storyline fascinated me. Soon, we both sat glued to the telly.

The movie was set in Mumbai when heavy rains had devastated it due to flooding in 2005.

The irony did not escape me. I thought to myself. What coincidence! Its been raining outside non-stop and here we are watching a movie where rain plays a major role.

In the movie, Mumbai is swamped and there's disaster and loss all around. The hero and the heroine are estranged lovers who bump into each other during this catastrophe. They see people struggling through a stormy night that threatens to take over the entire city, their fears and insecurities laid bare. The couple realises that there is no use fighting and bickering because no one knows just how transient and unpredictable this life can be.

Totally engrossed in the proceedings, I never imagined that only two days later, disaster and loss would not be confined to the safety of the screen. I would experience it for real.

Was the movie a mere coincidence or a premonition? I will never know.

Soon after it ended, Parth and I dozed off in the bed that was so soft and silky it made us feel like we were in the lap of our mothers, dreaming pleasant dreams.

4th September 2014

I am an early riser. On peeping outside the window at dawn, I saw the *Chinar*[68] trees standing still in the water pools that had formed because of the downpour.

With a cup of steaming hot tea, I sat near the window.

Looking at the *Chinars*[69], I felt they were whispering their melancholic tales to me. Through the window pane, wherever and however far my eyes went, I saw stillness and sadness hanging over the landscape. The long and dense line of trees presented a picture of dispirited desolation.

According to Abrahamic mythology, the Almighty formed this Earth in six days and seven nights without resting for a moment. Since he was creating the earth after heaven, he did not repeat the shortcomings of the zenith with earth.

Instead, he fashioned an enchanting place surrounded by hills, valleys, rivers, plains, seas, shores, rocks, caves and the most beautiful part, the woods––the dense forests, that were most admired by the Almighty himself. Then He allocated a fixed life span to every part of his creation––to the mountains, the rivers, the plains and the trees too.

Looking at the forlorn trees, I wondered what was it about the trees that they were made to stand alone to endure the pleasant and poignant moods of nature?

---

[68] *A deciduous tree*

[69] *A deciduous tree*

Perhaps Indian mythology could explain why the trees looked especially sombre.

Once God Brihaspati, the guru of *devas*[70], came to Lord Indra's court. Lord Indra, the rain god, didn't get up to pay him due respect. Lord Brihaspati couldn't stomach this insult and left in a huff. On realising his mistake, Lord Indra went to seek pardon, but couldn't find the guru.

Shukracharya, the guru of the demons who are *devas*'[71] rivals, became overjoyed. He immediately attacked and defeated them.

After the defeat, Brahmaji suggested the *devas*[72] conduct a *yagna*[73] to get forgiveness from their guru. *Rishi*[74] Vishwakarma presided over the *yagna*[75]. While he was conducting it, a demon approached him stealthily and asked him to chant their names also during the rituals so that the demons would be empowered too. Since Vishwakarma was the son of a demon mother, he agreed. As a result, the *devas*[76] didn't get enough powers.

Lord Indra flew into a rage on hearing the facts and cut off the three faces of Vishwakarma.

---

[70] *Gods*

[71] *Gods*

[72] *Gods*

[73] *a fire ritual involving sacrifice*

[74] *a sage*

[75] *a fire ritual involving sacrifice*

[76] *Gods*

Once again he was cursed for harming a saint.

He repented for thousands of years, but couldn't win pardon. Then Brahma came up with a plan to save him and divided his sin into four equal parts.

One part he gave to the Earth offsetting it with a blessing that any depression in the soil would automatically be levelled after a period of time.

The second part he gave to the water with the blessing that all the impurities will rise to the surface in the form of foam, keeping it crystal clear.

The third part he gave to women by giving them their menstruation but with the boon of producing babies.

And finally, the last part he gave to the trees with the blessing that if they dried or got uprooted, their roots would once again sprout to take the form of a giant and gigantic tree.

Thus, Lord Indra was freed from his sins.

But the way I saw it, the blessing proved to be a curse for the trees. They were trapped in immortality.

Deep in the woods, they have to spend time alone, without any companion or visitor, constantly struggling against the vagaries of weather.

As soon as a tree nears release from the cycle of birth and death, its seeds and roots sprout again! They never find freedom from the lonely spots they grow in. All over the world, history is a witness to trees as ancient as the Ramayana era or *Tretayuga*![77]

Looking outside the window in Gulmarg, I felt as if the raindrops were tears that the lonely trees were shedding incessantly begging for relief from the birth chakra.

But alas! No heed was paid to their appeal and the process of thunder, lightning and rain intensified. The clouds seemed to have taken an oath to empty themselves onto that beautiful valley that day.

Though no words were exchanged between us, I was able to understand the pain they were going through.

My heart cried for the nullity of Brahma's blessing. I longed to hug the desolate trees to provide a cloak to their naked bodies and give them some warmth.

They are also living creatures like us––they also take birth, eat, grow up and reproduce. They also cheer up in the spring season, but for how long?

Hardly do they start relishing the warmth, that melancholy autumn approaches and forcefully separates every leaf from the branches. The tree becomes bare again, bereft of its partners and children. There remains nobody to share its joy and sorrows, and it bears whatever is destined for it all alone.

---

[77] *Second of the four ages in Hindu mythology*

We human beings are lucky because we are allotted a fixed span of life –– say a hundred years at the most. But what about these dejected trees? They cannot go to annihilation by themselves. Unless the creator shows mercy, they have to linger on and on and on.

In those lonely moments, when I was sitting in the chair and gazing outside, I introspected as if we––the trees and me–– shared a similar fate. They are suffering from the pangs of loneliness as was I.

I tried to sooth them. "Like you, I also plead to God to relieve me from this birth and this earth. For how much longer will I have to struggle alone in all areas of life? I have already spent many years fighting my impoverishment tooth and nail. As I couldn't control my fate, I had to bow down to the desires of the creator like you do."

Ting, ting, ting…the doorbell disrupted my reverie.

I shook off the melancholic thoughts and got up to see who it was. Radhu brought the message that we had to be in the dining hall sharp at 9:30 a.m.

At the breakfast table, we met a couple with two beautiful daughters, Mannat and Mandira. Both were extremely charismatic and in western attire––shorts with tees.

Anju and I exchanged glances and Anju remarked, "How sparkling their skin is! Undoubtedly, they are real beauties." I nodded.

Anshu and Parth the chatterboxes, didn't utter a single word or talk to them. But the blush on their faces disclosed that they were appreciating the girls very much.

Radhu poked fun at them, "Oh! What happened? Why blushing? Okay! Choosing for yourselves, are you? Should I? Let the one in green shorts be for Anshu and the purple one for Parth."

Even Neha started pulling their leg, "I suppose you got the right matches. They look perfect for you. If you both agree, we can talk to their parents."

And we all started grinning naughtily.

Our kids befriended them. Mandira asked all to call her Mandy as she found that 'cool'.

We learned from them that they had been stranded in the hotel for the last three days due to the weather.

They hadn't been able to go out of the hotel as no taxi driver was ready to take the risk. They had heard of many landslides in the area in the last few days. They were also not sure if the weather would get better soon.

We were crestfallen at the news because if the rain didn't stop, we wouldn't be able to go out sightseeing.

We noticed all guests in the hotel were trying to kill time—some were playing cards, others surfing T.V. channels, some busy in deep conversation on different topics, some smoking, some enjoying music, others in dining hall, in the swimming pool or in the spa. All were forced to stay within the hotel confines.

After a few moments of disappointment, we managed to adjust our mood and looked for activities to do in the gorgeous property.

We soon found ourselves in the in-house swimming pool, which was quite big and luxurious. The water was lukewarm and all of us dived into it one by one.

Oh! How relaxing it was! Soon we were splashing about and enjoying ourselves. The water soothed and warmed our tired bodies. It was so refreshing and invigorating that we fell in love with it. But the attendant arrived and said he had to change the water, so we reluctantly climbed out of the pool after enjoying it for a couple of hours.

While others went off to enjoy the spa or busy themselves in other activities, I spent a good part of that day in the jacuzzi, luxuriating in the steam, sauna and shower. I felt like a queen who ruled over the entire sovereign.

What a lovely lavish feeling! It felt like after having broken thousands of bricks with my hands, my aching body was thrilled with the self-pampering. It was 'ME' time, and I was on cloud nine.

Around 3 p.m.

Radhu wished to eat some Chinese food but it wasn't available in the hotel. Manoj asked her to choose from the buffet but she was adamant. So he took all the kids to a nearby Chinese restaurant.

They returned after two hours. Talking about the conditions, they informed us that the road outside the hotel was blocked due to rain. Sanjay asked whether there was anything to worry about. Manoj nodded and said the situation did look grim. Still, we didn't bother much.

Late that night, we spent at least two hours in the dining hall with the same family. The night turned happening with the girls' presence.

We enjoyed the delicious dinner. As usual, Parth, Anshu and Radhu garnished the evening with their humorous leg pulling and general banter.

Then they got busy in having fun with other kids who were playing in the lobby. They divided all kids into two groups with Anshu heading one and Parth the other. Their motto was to make the kids fight with each other and the winner would be awarded well.

Parth would incite the kids, "If you beat the other boy, I will give you a chocolate and if you push him hard I will give you a packet of chips."

Anshu, on the other side, was also doing the same. "Bravo my boys! You can do it, just go and push him on the mattress. Go boy, go!"

Parth, "Dare you come here! Touch if you can…my hero will break your bones."

The games continued till the teenagers had made all the kids cry as they didn't give them either chocolates or chips. They left saying, "You didn't play well. Show your skills better tomorrow and we will give you double the chocolates and chips. Time to sleep now…your Moms are calling. Good night! We will wait for you tomorrow morning to start the game again."

They retired into their rooms laughing to their hearts content. We all, too, went to our beds.

It was still raining outside.

5th September 2014

The day started on a very joyous note as I received a lot of calls and messages from my dear students wishing me 'Happy Teachers Day'.

If I had been in Delhi, I would have received many gifts and cards loaded with lovely messages. Even though I missed the face-to-face interaction with my students, I loved how the day began with so many warm wishes.

Their messages made me feel loved and valued, even in far-away Gulmarg.

I got so lost in reading the messages and responding to them that it slipped my mind we were supposed to get ready soon for our drive back to Srinagar.

I dressed hurriedly and came out of the room to begin the journey by the same Tempo Traveller with Hasan. We had to leave Gulmarg soon as rumours were rife in the hotel that the weather could deteriorate further and then it would become impossible to reach Srinagar.

So we readily agreed to the suggestion of leaving Gulmarg as soon as possible.

At 10 a.m.

It was raining heavily. We were enjoying the drive through the rain-soaked valley. The regret of not getting an opportunity to see the soul-stirring sights of Gulmarg plagued our hearts but somehow we managed to check our sense of disappointment as there was no other alternative.

Oh! The rain! What kind of drops are these that are not ready to pause even for a second but are getting fiercer and bolder by the hour, I thought.

But as long as we were not getting drenched, it was OK. Through the windows of the Tempo, we could see the land all around shadowed by a blanket of clouds and cascading rain. We were in a jolly mood and cracked jokes at the mad weather. At the same time, we were astonished at the sheets of water dropping from the heavens above.

What irked us were only our altered plans and discomfort and nothing else!

On the way back, the scene on the roads was very worrisome. Deep-rooted trees, which had seemed unshakeable only two days ago, had been overcome by the joint force of tiny droplets. I found it unbelievable that such fragile drops had such mighty force.

Looking at those trees I was reminded of the words 'Unity is Strength'. I had heard them many times before but hadn't realised the message in them.

One drop of water can hardly produce any significant change on earth, but as soon as many of them join heads, their power becomes unchallengeable. That week in Kashmir, they had united to submerge the valley under water.

We have witnessed the pleasing side of the rain and have read alluring tales of its beauty.

Rain, the daughter of the sea, descends as silver pearls to adorn the valleys and quench the thirst of the parched land. Its arrival is celebrated not only by living beings, but also by the tiniest particles of the dust that are enlivened by its drops.

But we were now witnessing the other side of gossamer rain. How can these delicate droplets take the guise of a flood? Can these little wonders create such havoc?

As we moved further, we saw how powerful they can get.

Heavy rocks washed away by the rain blocked the roads. Tall *Chinars*[78], whose doleful ballads I was singing a day before when I saw them from my room, were now lying uprooted.

We heard that the flood had washed away more than a thousand villages in the valley.

The connecting flyover between Srinagar and Gulmarg (the same one by which we had entered this paradise) had fallen into the Jhelum river!

This news hit us like a bolt from the blue! We found it impossible to believe that such a colossal structure had buckled under without any violent force being applied to it.

As a result of that crash, there was no choice for us but to use narrow, dangerous passes to reach Srinagar.

For the first time, we became a little serious about our predicament.

Hasan––hats off to him––was a specimen of alertness and attentiveness. He knew how to drive safely even under those critical conditions.

He took us through those treacherous passes with hardly a frown on his brow. Whenever needed, he turned and reversed the car at such speed that we all screamed.

---

[78] *A deciduous tree*

Unlike us, he was his normal self even under such stressful conditions. The road was so uneven and he was driving so fast that we felt as if we were swinging on Columbus rides.

Hasan hardly attended to our advice to drive slow and safe. He just kept humming Kashmiri tunes and dealt with each deadly turn just as he would deal with a normal road.

At length, we escaped the diabolic dirt roads and breathed a sigh of relief. But it was not to last too long.

We had just crossed those narrow, stony passes with our hearts in our mouths and had thanked the deity that he had spared us. But we did not realise it was not the end of the tale.

In fact, it was the beginning of a catastrophe.

Driving ahead, we witnessed the damage caused by the vicious flood. We couldn't believe our eyes that only two days ago, the roads on which we had travelled in such a jolly mood, were nowhere to be seen.

The area had transformed into an enormous water body, which was flowing at a furious speed overrunning whatever came in its path––humans, houses, huts, trees, roads, cattle, electric poles or any other luxury of the world.

It didn't discriminate at all and swallowed everything in its gigantic, hungry maw.

We saw a very sad scene. Thousands of people had become shelter less. Many were crying bitterly at the loss of their homes, property, cattle and other belongings, which had been carried away by the flood.

The calamity brought on by water had left its cruel mark everywhere.

I saw an old woman trying hard to catch her aluminium plate that was being carried away by the running water. The sight was heart rending. Men were standing speechless watching their huts and houses crumbling so easily in the muddy tides.

It was a picture of sorrow all around. In the safety of the Tempo Traveller we shook our heads in sympathy and wondered, "What will these people do now? Will they get something to eat? How will they spend the night on chilly and flooded roads without any warmth? What will their future be? How will they console themselves for the irreparable loss of their homes and their little wealth?"

All eyes were brimming with tears at the devastation.

Suddenly, our tyres got stuck in the mud and our Tempo was unable to move. Hasan asked us to get down. Then he requested some people to help him get the Traveller out of the mud.

Though they themselves were reeling from the tragedy of losing all they had, people helped us get the vehicle out of the slush.

They also told Hasan not follow the route we were on as there had been an incident ahead. Some electric wires had fallen into water. A little girl, who had been standing on the terrace of her house, lost her balance and accidentally fell into the water below. She got electrocuted and met her death within minutes.

The story was more than enough to strike terror in our hearts. Absolute silence descended in the Tempo. Though it was already 2 p.m. and we were hungry, nobody asked for food.

The question before us was what way to take to Srinagar as we were totally cut off from the city.

We were left with no option but to follow the risk-laden paths that went through the forest area. These passes through the dense jungle scared the living daylights out of us. With every turn, we felt our vehicle would slide into the muddy slush on the side of the path and get stuck.

It took several hours for us to reach the city and each minute of that journey was a tense one.

But somehow we managed to reach Srinagar.

It was raining in the city too, but we were happy to be out of danger. Though the water was flowing all over on the roads, for us Delhites it was a normal sight because we see that sort of thing every rainy season. In Delhi, I love to drive my car through the small pools that form on the roads to create a splash.

Seeing such a familiar sight in Srinagar, our spirits revived and we clicked pictures of the waterlogged roads.

Instead of taking the flowing water seriously, we began enjoying it. We promptly forgot the tragedy we had witnessed outside the city and the trauma of the treacherous roads we had endured only a few hours back. All we wanted was to enjoy our trip since we had already lost two days in Gulmarg, our precious time marred by the wickedness of the rainy weather. We broke into complaints against God for confining us to the hotel in Gulmarg and not letting us enjoy the legendary beauty of that place.

Here is a confession –– as soon as I felt safe, I transformed and didn't consider it worthy to spend any more moments pondering over the agony of the flood victims we had seen only a while back.

Within a matter of minutes, normal life completely took over, erasing all impressions of the suffering we had just left behind!

We soon reached Sarovar Portico, a hotel on a small hill. But as soon as the manager showed us the rooms, all our joy evaporated.

The rooms were very small and cleanliness wasn't up to our standards. We had just come back from Khyber, the five star hotel! We had tasted royal treatment. How could we settle for these dingy cells now?

All rebelled against staying there, especially us women. The men were almost ready to adjust but we rebelled against the idea without considering that the men were looking at things practically.

When we called the manager, he added to our woes when he said he could allot only three rooms to us, even though we had booked four rooms from Delhi.

All the payments had been made. We had all the right to be angry and shout at the manager. And we did. Though we complained and screamed at him, he remained calm and dealt with us patiently.

He offered us the option of changing the hotel, if we wanted. At the same time he confused us by saying that under those circumstances, no accommodation would be easily available in Srinagar.

Even the waiters at the place weren't very attentive. We had ordered *kahwa* but it was served only after an hour or so. After relishing it, we decided that Anju, Parth, Anshu and I would go in the Tempo with Hasan to find a better hotel in nearby areas.

Sanjay wanted to shift into The Lalit, another five star, as he prefers to stay in quality hotels. On his persuasion, we went to see The Lalit, which was a fine specimen of luxury and grandeur.

Undoubtedly, it was a place where we would have no second thoughts about staying. We found ourselves again in a dreamland and forgot all our mental and physical tiredness.

But when got to know the tariff, Manoj and I backed out saying that it would double our budgets. Sanjay tried his best to convince us and also to get a deal from the hotel.

The negotiations ate up around two hours of our time, but we were not lucky enough to get a workable deal there. Only two rooms were available, so once again we set off in search of a hotel.

This time we took the lead to look for a better and a reasonable hotel. Hasan took us to many but none fascinated us as they were not to our taste.

We went back to Sarovar Portico. All of us were dog-tired and were craving for a cozy room at the earliest. We sat demoralised in the lobby of the Sarovar.

Though it was a matter of being room less for only a short while, with a guarantee of finding a room either now or after a few hours, it compelled me to mull over the fact how such a minor uncertainty had depressed us so much.

What about those peddlers and beggars who don't have permanent homes and are condemned to shiver through uncountable chilly nights on the roadside.

None of us go close to them or attend to their needs. Even when we see poor women begging with naked kids in their arms, we pay no heed. We don't even pause to let our eyes see the painful sight. We just ignore and move on.

And here, just a few hours of not knowing about where we will stay had punctured our spirits.

Finally, the hotel manager offered us accommodation in a newly built hotel CH2 on the Broadway Road, near Jhelum river. We hurried to see the hotel. It was not very luxurious, but we decided to stay there anyway.

There were many valid and concrete reasons for that decision. The most significant was that we were terribly tired. Also, it was getting very dark and the weather condition hadn't improved. Things did not look very secure. Moreover, we were dying of hunger.

So we checked in and got our rooms assigned.

Though Khyber and CH2 could not be compared in any sense, the situation demanded that we bring down our standards and adjust accordingly. The proverb 'Beggars are not choosers' proved to be correct in those hours.

After settling in, we went to have dinner in Krishna *Dhaba*[79], one of the most famous *dhabas*[80] at Lal Bagh Road.

We ordered a number of dishes and ate hungrily as every dish, especially *Rajma Chawal*[81] and *Kari Chawal*[82], were extremely tasty. But we didn't feel satisfied. Our stomachs

---

[79] *small roadside eatery*

[80] *small roadside eatery*

[81] *Rice and beans*

[82] *Rice and chickpea flours and curd preparation*

demanded more so we stuffed ourselves with many desserts and drinks.

Lal Bagh Road was very crowded and full of life as it was the main market area near Dal Lake. There were many tourists even in the late hours, all looking happy and gay.

There was an emporium adjacent to Krishna *Dhaba*[83]. We went there to have a look at the Kashmiri goods being sold, but very soon Sanjay commanded us to get back to hotel as it was almost midnight. So, we all trooped back to CH2.

The rain continued to come down hard.

---

[83] *small roadside eatery*

CHAPTER 8

6th September 2014

Though the room was a very ordinary one, Parth and I had a comfortable night. In the morning, I was craving to have a cup of tea but to my dismay there was no kettle in the room.

To divert my mind I focussed on getting ready for breakfast as we had a long list of things to do that day.

The dining hall of CH2, though small, offered a delicious spread of breakfast. We relished every bite of *dosas[84], *idlis[85] and *paranthas[86] followed by cup after cup of cardamom-flavoured tea.

This is where we first met Mr. and Mrs. Dharmendra Mehra——at the dining table. We had a good, friendly chat with them.

Mr. Mehra told us his father was a film producer and had produced the movie 'Kismat' in his younger years. I was delighted to meet him! The song 'Kajra Mohhabatwala'

---

[84] *rice and lentil savoury pancakes*
[85] *steamed cake of rice and lentil*
[86] *stuffed flatbread, usually shallow fried*

from this very movie is one of my all-time favourites and I love to hear it on a loop.

Sanjay took a keen interest in the couple and spoke with them for long. Mrs. Mehra told us that they had bought shawls, suits, handicrafts etc. from a particular emporium and if we wished to shop, there was no emporium better than that. The quality, the range, the pricing——all was top notch according to them.

Mr. Mehra also broke to us the news that the water level had been rising continuously in Srinagar. He told us that they were heading to Gulmarg that day. He was very eager to get there, as according to him, Gulmarg would be a safer place in this weather than Srinagar.

We told him that the move would be very unwise and unsafe. We shared with them the details of the damage due to flood we had witnessed on our way from Gulmarg. We also narrated the harrowing tale of our escape. Only we know how we had narrowly missed being stranded in the deluge!

They were shocked to hear these reports because they had absolutely no idea what had happened and that the situation was so bad!

We also told them about the connecting flyover between Srinagar and Gulmarg. Jhelum river had overrun it due to which electricity, phone, television, and radio connections had been lost.

Mr. Mehra ruefully told us that since the day they had reached Kashmir, they had been stranded in the rain and were forced to stay within CH2. It had been two days almost and they hadn't done anything except shop. Now they were bored to the core and wanted to make a quick exit from this place.

But following our update of the conditions in Gulmarg, they decided to visit nearby places in Srinagar instead.

And we planned to shop for shawls, stoles, suits, purses, and other local craft items. We took Mr. Mehra's warning of continuously rising water in Srinagar casually, even after witnessing so much destruction with our own eyes.

We had spent a lot of time, effort and money on the trip, and felt like caged pigeons due to the weather.

We wanted to break all barriers and soar high,
Despite the thundering and stormy sky.

Though we knew danger was close at hand, we felt we had suffered enough already and were justified in making most of our time left. In fact, we were convinced we deserved every bit of enjoyment since rain had already forced us to stay indoors in Gulmarg.

The hotel staff assured us that there had never been any danger in the capital for ages. Floods and rains, though usual in the valley, affect only low-lying villages.

They added that the city had always been safe. Even their great grandparents had never heard or spoken of any flood in the city in the last century. They told us we could go shopping without any worries.

Just then Sanjay got a call from his father from Delhi who was worried about the worsening conditions in Kashmir. He had seen dire reports on news channels and urged Sanjay to come back with everyone. Sanjay told him that TV channels were as usual hyperventilating and assured his father there was nothing to worry about and the city was safe.

More confidence in our plans came via the views of many locals that the city was secure and no water could ever breach its boundaries.

Convinced by these inputs, we unanimously decided to stay on in Srinagar and not to go back to Delhi. None of us at that time wanted to pay the slightest attention to any suggestions to the contrary. We were an enthusiastic gang ready to encounter any pleasant or unpleasant situation with gusto.

But just to be doubly sure, we once again spoke to a few members of the hotel staff about how safe going out in this weather would be. They laughed at us as if we had cracked a joke. This was just the signal we needed to turn our steps towards the city and explore and shop to our heart's content.

So, defying all ominous warnings from the heavens above, off we went very excitedly to the emporium suggested by Mr. Mehra to shop for the world famous Pashmina shawls.

As we trooped into the shop, the owners greeted us with great warmth and showed us a fabulous range of woollen suits, pashmina shawls, stoles, purses and other items.

The shopkeepers arranged for us the tastiest tea and we gulped down a good number of cups while they displayed pure *toosh* shawls at subsidised rates.

The shawls were priced between Rs. 30K to 3lacs a piece. Manoj and Neha wanted to buy a 30K shawl for their father. But Anju stopped them saying, "First, we'll go to the shawl seller's house who we had promised to visit on the first day of our arrival."

Remembering the seller who had showed up at the Welcome Group *shikara*, we did not buy the shawls but picked up plenty of other things from the emporium.

As soon as we wrapped up there, we headed to the shawl seller's house, which was around 10kms from there. It was in one of the low-lying areas of the city.

It was not a very smart idea to visit the risky area during the rains, but so as not to spoil our mood, Sanjay agreed to let us go on this shopping adventure.

All through the way, the rain got fiercer. But Hasan knew all the short cuts and took us to the seller's home.

Though it was small, the house was neatly maintained. It was a Muslim family, very hospitable and cultured. The owner, Ahmed *miyan*[87], welcomed us warmly and showed us a great variety of shawls and stoles.

I was astonished to see that they kept their treasured stock of shawls tied in a few cotton bundles. Each bundle had almost 50-70 shawls ranging from 5K to 10lacs per piece. The approximate value of those bundles would be in crores! Even so, the whole family seemed to be very simple and humble.

Ahmed *miyan*[88] and his son Abid unwrapped more expensive shawls, some of which usually took almost two years to be ready for sale. They were all very alluring in their own ways with different patterns of embroidery that was simply irresistible.

I couldn't help wondering how these people work so patiently! How they manage to create delicate motifs using a single thread in different colours to create a shading effect. They must be burning the midnight oil to achieve such levels of perfection.

Ahmed *miyan*[89] told us that many homes in Kashmir have small-scale embroidery industries with workers investing their time and souls to produce these world-class exquisite beauties. He said many movie stars come to them to buy shawls and add to their collections.

---

[87] *respectful epithet in urdu meaning sir, mister*

[88] *respectful epithet in urdu meaning sir, mister*

[89] *respectful epithet in urdu meaning sir, mister*

I bought one shawl worth 27K and Anju bought one for 35K and many stoles. But the desire to possess some more of these wonderful woollens didn't leave our souls easily.

We craved to add a few more pieces to our collection. We wanted to make the best use of our Kashmir trip, even though there was hardly any need for buying more.

While we sat there basking in the beauty of the shawls, and struggling to contain our desires, Ahmed *miyan's*[90] neighbours came twice to warn that continuous rain had taken a serious turn and they wanted to talk to him regarding what precautionary measures should be taken.

But both times Ahmed *miyan*[91] told Abid, "You see what the matter is. Go and tell *bhaijaan* that I'm busy with customers. I'll be out shortly."

Manoj asked him, "Ahmed *miyan*[92], sab theek hai na?" to which he replied, "Ji huzoor, sab khairiyat."

He was not ready to shift his focus from his customers even for a second.

Sanjay and Manoj started warning us that it was already very late and we had to traverse a long and risky way back. They wanted to leave at the earliest.

---

[90] *respectful epithet in urdu meaning sir, mister*
[91] *respectful epithet in urdu meaning sir, mister*
[92] *respectful epithet in urdu meaning sir, mister*

Though we were also aware of the deteriorating conditions, we were completely under the enchanting spell of Ahmed *miyan's*[93] treasure.

God knows what happened to us and we couldn't take the alarming signs and warnings seriously. We simply kept requesting Sanjay and Manoj to grant us a few minutes more and convinced them to stay on for a bit longer.

It was not that we did not understand the depth and seriousness of their statements but as soon as we made up our minds to put a full stop to the shopping, *miyanji* would exhibit another eye-catching collection saying, "Sister, we are not compelling you to buy anything. We just want you to have a look at these marvellous pieces and in the future if you plan to visit again, then you can buy them."

Trust me, when he opened that bundle, we were glued to our seats once again, mesmerised by what he had just displayed and overcome with the temptation to possess those as well. All pieces were such fabulous specimens of great craftsmanship!

Another factor in our staying so long was that this was Neha and Anju's first visit to the valley. They had come prepared to shop a lot. A Lot! And Pashmina shawls were the ultimate prize they were after.

---

[93]   *respectful epithet in urdu meaning sir, mister*

We had not only lost so many days without having bought what we came for, Ahmed *'miyan*[94] had yet not displayed that ONE shawl they had dreamt of buying. Everyone who loves clothes craves for that one piece that takes their breath away!

Also, it is almost next to impossible to ever be satisfied with our purchases and difficult to stop looking and digging for better deals.

While Sanjay and Manoj were getting visibly agitated at the delay, their better halves Neha and Anju were in the grips of a shopping fever that evening.

So was I, I must admit.

I was reminded of the Garden of Eden. While Adam cautioned Eve not to go alone into the woods lest she get trapped, Eve overruled her husband's advice and went alone into the forest where Satan tempted her to taste the fruit of the forbidden tree. She couldn't resist his advances and ate it, disobeying her husband Adam's plea and God's command.

My nieces and I behaved like true descendants of Eve that evening. A crazy streak of temptation took over, so much so that it could jeopardize our safety.

Only when it grew terribly dark, did we think of getting up and rushing back to our hotel. But at the last moment also, Ahmed *'miyan*[95] offered to show us a unique variety of

---

[94] *respectful epithet in urdu meaning sir, mister*
[95] *respectful epithet in urdu meaning sir, mister*

shawls on the following day. We decided to revisit at sharp 10 a.m. the next day.

Why were we being so hoggish?

Why didn't we have a hold on the horses?

Each one of us is materialistic and we use our shrewd minds to acquire whatever we can. We leave no stone unturned to gratify our lusts.

We forget that our life is short and there is no use of hoarding so much heedlessly.

We are unable to enjoy even half of what we have accumulated in our lifetimes! We come face to face with death which arrives without prior notice, and with whom we have to go along empty handed.

Though everyone is aware of this blunt fact of life, the madness of accumulating wealth has continued over the civilisations and centuries and will continue indefinitely.

But what is the use of storing so much wealth?

Why don't we understand that we simply are nothing before God's will? He can create or destroy the whole world by raising a single brow making all of mankind submit to his command.

Then why don't we just surrender to the deity and stay satisfied with whatever has been granted to us?

But we just don't. We make all efforts to fulfil our wanton wishes ignoring whether they are beneficial or harmful for us.

In this trip also, we had overruled our own group members' advice two times and consequently put our lives at risk.

Firstly, we had refused to stay at Sarovar Portico, a hotel on a hillside and hence safe, and landed at CH2 instead which was right behind the Jhelum river.

Secondly, after staying for too long in Ahmed *miyan's*[96] house, we had to face a harrowing time on our way back as water had clogged all narrow lanes.

The streets had become quite dirty and there was no proper drainage system, which would allow the water to pass. Men and children had come out of their houses and were discussing whether the situation could get more dangerous.

Our car was parked on the main road, far from *miyanji's* house. We had to walk through muddy water that came right up to our knees.

Manoj as usual lost his cool, "Because of your stupidity, we have to walk through this stinking water. Our clothes and shoes have already become muddy. Now at least hold these costly bags carefully. And stop moving like tortoises and be fast!"

---

[96] *respectful epithet in urdu meaning sir, mister*

Just after this, Aaru began pulling Neha's shirt, "Mummy, I don't want to walk anymore. Pick me up. My jeans are wet and I want to pee."

He kept crying and howling.

Radhu rebuked Aaru, "Its not just your jeans. Everybody is wet. Now shut up and walk peacefully!"

Somehow we crossed the flooded street and reached the car. The entire area looked unsafe and we entreated Hasan to hurry up.

Hasan, who after that tomato incident had not been saying too much to us, just focussed on driving. He had to take many turns to avoid the flooded and slippery roads. It took us a very long time to get back to CH2, but finally we made it.

Now we realised that if we had listened to Sanjay and Manoj's pleas, we would have been saved the trouble. But it was too late to regret now. What's the use crying over spilt milk?

On our way back, it continued raining non-stop and the water level on the roads kept rising.

At 10 p.m.

After dinner, we gathered in Anju's room to have a look at each other's purchases. It was wonderful going over all the expensive and great shopping we had finally managed.

We actually never get bored of it and we had a good time discussing every piece till almost midnight.

Around 12:15 a.m.

We went back to our respective rooms and slept soundly, blissfully unaware of the fact that only within a few hours, our life was going to be turned upside down and a new horrifying chapter was going to be written for the city of Srinagar.

I hadn't been able to sleep for even an hour when I was disturbed by the din in the corridor.

I marched out in anger to see who was making so much noise, saw strange men in *kurta pyjamas* talking in loud voices, quickly bolted the door shut out of fear and called the reception to find out what on earth was going on!

Our Shyam baba Khatu Waale

My parents – Mr & Mrs Kashi Ram Aggarwal

My parents-in-law- Mr & Mrs Sneh Gupta

Anil and me on our wedding day- 23rd Jan, 1987

In Shimla Dec, 1987

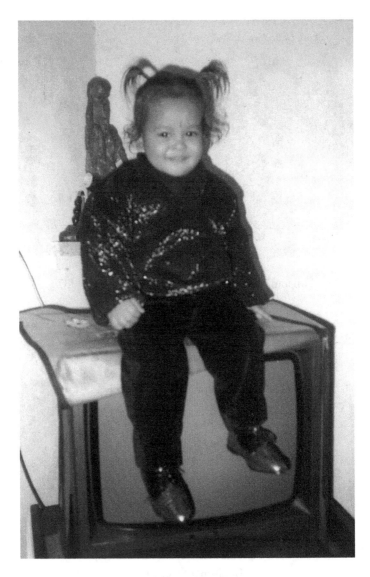

Kashish of 3 years

Parth of 3 years

My first trip to Kashmir 1998

We all at Nishat Garden

At Pahalgaon guarded by army men

Loving moments- Kashish & Parth

Anil singing at Talkatora Stadium on Dec, 2000

We both at Same function

Anil with Mrs Shiela Dixit

Me and Kashish at a Christian wedding

Happy Times holidaying at Rohtang Pass, Manali

Kashish and Parth at Manali

Me and Kashish at Rohtang Pass, Manali

Me and my two beloved sons

Our group to Kashmir on 2nd September, 2014

Myself

Parth and me-at nishat garden

Our captain- Mr. Sanjay Mittal

Flooded villages on our way back from Gulmarg

CH2 Hotel

The views from CH2 terrace

Local Kashmiris in their own boat

Myself at army base camp

Myself at army base camp

Parth at army base camp

Army base camp hospital

We all in the queue down from Jayesta Mata Temple

Queue to enter in Helipad's gate

Crowd at chopper's line

Kashish, Myself and Parth happily united again.

CHAPTER 9

9th September 2014

10 a.m.

After waiting for the boats for so long with no success, the tired mass was sitting in a mood of deep dejection and despair. Whenever we peeped out of the windows, the weather and the water both looked menacing. The rising water looked too brutal to be bridled.

Suddenly, a boat arrived! A whoop of joy went up.

Our battered spirits were rekindled with the flame of optimism. We turned our attention to the shrieking, groaning and fearful sounds that accompanied its arrival.

The second level of our survival game had begun.

11 a.m.

As soon as the words, *"Jaldi aaoo, boat aa gayi hai!"*[97] were heard, a tide of people, who had till then been squatting or

---

[97] *Come fast! The boat has arrived*

standing resignedly, sprung up and began the mad dash to the room on the second floor.

We pushed each other like ferocious animals to get to that same den of frosty water where we had spent the previous night.

The very thought of wading into that dreaded pool shrivelled up our insides. But passing through that tunnel was the only way of staying alive. So all ran for it like trapped animals trying to escape certain death.

I moved ahead gathering the last ounces of stamina left in my body. But I had to stop suddenly because my ankle wound opened up and started bleeding. People just rushed past me, pushing me aside.

No one was ready to let that golden opportunity slip through their fingers. A desperate struggle as to who would go first began. People were pulling, pushing and hitting each other, trying to get their family members to move ahead.

But when the army men announced that they would take women and small kids only, the crowd had to allow us to enter the boat one by one.

As I was the last one in the line, the boatman pulled me in very unceremoniously.

The entire operation was being carried out briskly and mechanically. Like robots, the army men arranged most women and children in the boat quickly.

But the moment I sat in the boat and regained my breath, I realised that my Parth wasn't there. He was still stranded somewhere at the back. I started looking around wildly for him. I held the boatman by his arm and kept on shaking him furiously and begged him to wait for my son. My heart was thumping fast and I was weeping uncontrollably. I had become an emotional wreck by then with problems raining on us one after the other and being separated from Parth was the last straw.

At that moment, I felt these miseries would never end. Why did my family members get separated from me time and again? First my husband took leave from this earth, then, in this calamity Kashish was back in Delhi. But now the limits of my tolerance were breached when Parth got lost in the mob leaving me alone at a time when I was most vulnerable.

The whole world seemed to have ended. My head screamed—Why is this so? Everything and everyone I cherish gets forcefully separated from me. I felt completely defeated by luck!

Words deny to draw a picture of those morose moments.

"No more!" screamed every cell in my body. I cannot let this happen! I must put an end to this!

I gripped the boatman and shouted, almost commanding him, *"Mera beta! Usse bachaoo!"*[98]

---

[98] *Save my son!*

But Parth wasn't there to be seen. I kept screaming louder and louder and began to pray, "For heaven's sake, Lord! Show me a glimpse of my son."

Nobody was sure whether the people left behind would be able to reach the army camp or not.

My heart hardened into a rebel. I said to the boatmen, "I will not go without my son."

I wasn't sure whether my stubbornness would bear any fruit or not but I kept interrupting whatever they were doing.

I don't know how it happened, but my prayers were answered and Parth appeared at the edge of the platform just in the nick of time. On spotting me, he lost control over his emotions and started mumbling, "Mumma! Mumma!"

He stretched his arms to reach out. He is very sensitive and loves and cares for me dearly. When he saw me in such a miserable state, screaming and crying, he tried to reach out to console me but in that attempt almost walked off the platform without realising what he was doing and almost fell into the water.

When I saw him in water, I panicked and everything began to black out. I screamed aloud to the army men to save him.

The boatmen, realising the seriousness of the situation, threw their ropes to him and asked the milling mob to let Parth hold it. Two boys, who were standing on the platform, got a hold on Parth and somehow managed to push him and help him find some room in the already stuffed boat.

Finally he was with me! I felt I hit the jackpot.
Oh, the moment!

Tears in our eyes, we threw ourselves in each other's arms. I clasped him and felt complete. We both felt we had been bestowed all the bounties of the world.

But the reunion provided only momentary pleasure and solace to us. The situation had undoubtedly improved and our sense of anguish was lulled for a few fleeting minutes. But now our group was split into two.

All men, except Parth, were in the building while the rest of us were in the boat heading for an unknown destination.

The boat started moving.

Miseries, though, were not done flocking to us. On moving just a little ahead, after about 5 minutes, we felt a big jerk and we all lurched to one side. We heard a screeching sound and everyone questioned at once, "What was that?"

The boat handlers were also flummoxed as to what had happened. Suddenly, we saw a small spout of water on the floor of the boat right in the middle! We realised the boat had perhaps collided with something under the water level— a car, a tin shed or a house top —something sharp edged had ripped a hole in the boat. The hole must have been a centimetre or two. Later we spotted a few more on the sides.

Immediately, water started gushing in and we found ourselves caught between the devil and the deep blue sea.

The crew shouted for help. They tried to catch the attention of passing lifeboats. But since they were too far away, they were either unable to hear us or perhaps did not pay attention as they had become accustomed to people screaming for help all around. Hence, no boat responded to our SOS call.

Danger was escalating with every passing moment. So was panic. In no time at all, a whole lot of water had flooded into the boat. It had reached halfway between our ankles and our knees.

The boat was wobbling wildly and losing balance. If the inflow was not checked immediately, then there was no doubt the boat would capsize and we would drown. We found ourselves staring death in the face yet again.

Luckily, the army men found a canvass in the boat. They quickly ripped it into small pieces and stuffed them in the gaping holes.

Water stopped flowing in.

They instructed us to throw water outside the boat. Since only one mug was available on the boat, all of us including little Aarav, cupped water in our hands and tried draining it off the boat one fistful at a time. We kept doing it like maniacs for about 15 minutes.

We started picking up stuff floating by––plates, wood, rags, anything––twisted it into something shaped like a cup and used that to collect water and throw it out.

When the situation stabilized a bit, the men tried moving the boat forward. It had barely moved an inch or two when another loud screech was felt. A fresh hole appeared in the front portion of the boat. A *jawan* quickly removed his jacket and stuffed it into this gap before water could rush in from there.

The army men immediately sensed our panic and calmed us saying that if we did not move too much, we would cross the patch where we were stuck. The journey ahead then would be smooth. God bless their good sense and spirits!

Their calm demeanour gave us confidence. They tried once again and moved the boat ahead very slowly. This time we were able to make progress, perhaps because the boat had freed itself of whatever it had got tangled with.

The rest of the journey was undertaken very, very slowly. They steered the boat with great caution.

On the way, we saw the whole vale had drowned. Only the upper most parts of the tall trees were visible. We saw animals floating nearby and moaning for help. One little puppy was trying to stay afloat near our boat, half dead. I requested the army man, "Why don't you pick this little puppy also?" He very politely explained that the boat was already overcrowded and damaged and could sink any moment. Their task was to save human beings first.

He also broke the news to us that the evacuation process had been delayed because the whole army camp had sunk in the flood and more than 800 *jawans* were being saved first so that they could help with the rescue work.

He told us that our boat was over the army camp! Army boards, dresses, boots and other things could be seen floating and bobbing up and down on the water.

This was SHOCKING! How could this be possible? Can an army camp, which is supposed to be the safest place in the city, also drown? The *jawans* who save others, were being saved by others!

I found this fact too difficult to comprehend.

He further told us that many *jawans* were still stranded and the evacuation process was in full swing. And the rescued *jawans*, despite ill health, immediately joined the rescue operations. One *jawan* can save many people hence his life is precious not only for him but also for the entire nation.

We were wondering that if the army camp had drowned, where were they taking us. Clearing our doubts the boatman informed, "Madam, the main base camp is quite big and at a sufficient height. It is capable of housing almost half of Srinagar. That's the safest place which is beyond any threat of flood."

Were we relieved to hear that!

The army camp wasn't very far away but due to the damage to our boat, it took us quite a while to get there.

Around 1 p.m.

Finally, our boat hit the shore. With the help of the army staff, everyone was helped out of the damaged boat very gently. They spoke to us with warm and helped us step out.

The feeling of dry and secure land under our feet again can in no way be described. We staggered in utter astonishment.

We had crossed an ocean and were safe ashore! It seemed almost unbelievable. We all hugged each other.

At the camp, our names and addresses were registered so that they could put them out on T.V., radio and Internet in the lists of people rescued.

We felt secure among soldiers.

Completely worn out, we sat down on the ground. The staff gave us a small quantity of black tea to drink. On sipping the hot beverage, the feel…Oh, my good Lord! It is beyond description.

For the last two days we hadn't eaten anything except a piece of biscuit. With tea, we were given a few *namakpare*[99]

---

[99] *Deep fried savoury snack*

as well. We swallowed them immediately as we were dying of hunger.

At that time, the number of rescued was not very high. Only the infirm, the injured locals and their families could be seen.

But new tourists were arriving as more boats unloaded their cargoes at the camp. The army was trying to send them immediately via choppers to the army airport at Srinagar so that they could catch flights to their destinations and be cleared out of the valley safely.

An officer arrived and announced that there were two seats vacant in the next chopper and if there was a two-member family, it could fly out with that chopper.

They realised that my family (Parth and I) were around, so they asked us to board the chopper.

Afterwards, we could take a flight to Delhi. They explained to me that by the time more boats arrived, the number of tourists would increase and then getting a ride to the airport would become very difficult.

I refused.

They urged us not to miss the opportunity.

They reasoned, "Ma'am, you aren't taking this calamity seriously. You do not understand the enormity of the catastrophe. But we know that the following hours will be harrowing. In just a few hours more, thousands of people from all over Kashmir, locals and tourists, will flood the camp.

It will be unwise not to return to safety immediately."

They were sure that if I did not grab the opportunity now, I would very soon be begging for just such a chance to escape.

Even Parth asked me not to let the lucky chance pass, as it would lessen the burden on Sanjay *jijaji* who had been shouldering the responsibility of our group all on his own. And if two people were safe, then he'd only have to worry about seven instead of nine.

But I was the eldest in the group. I could not shake the sense of my responsibility to the younger lot. I refused the offer as I couldn't leave others alone to face the trauma.

The officers approached us again after 10 minutes and insisted, "Ma'am, the chopper is about to leave, you still have the time to decide if you want to go. You can send any two members."

Anju and Neha also refused to go as they didn't want to leave without their husbands. And I stuck to my earlier decision. I would not go alone and nothing could make me change my mind. So, I refused yet again.

We came together and we will go back together. That was my final decision.

The chopper left without us.

Around 2 p.m.

When we had settled at the camp, we started envisioning the condition of our dear ones in Delhi.

What was their mental condition? How was my Kashish consoling himself? Who would be giving him solace? He must be trying tooth and nail to save his mother and brother. He would be glued to his laptop to scan the list of the rescued.

Oh, he must be feeling so alone!

I prayed to Lord Krishna, "Kashish has always stood strong like an iron pillar to protect us. He has always advised and assisted me in all matters. But how helpless he must be feeling in these hours of dire need. Kindly be by my son's side. He doesn't have any shoulders to cry upon."

My thoughts raced back to 2002.

Kashish, Parth and I had gone to the market to buy groceries. Kashish and I were totally engrossed in the shopping. When we were done and came out of the shop, we found Parth missing. I was gripped with panic.

We ran around in all directions to search for him. He was just six years old and hardly knew anything about home addresses or phone numbers. Even after hunting for him for a long time, we couldn't find him.

195

Kashish consoled me throughout that ordeal, "Mummy, we'll find him. I'll make everything okay. Don't loose heart. Let's go to the Police Station."

We went to the Police Station and found Parth sitting there and crying. Kashish ran and held him in his arms, sobbing, *"Mere bhai tune to meri jaan hi nikal di[100]…you okay?"*

He kissed and hugged him. I stood there surprised at how mature Kashish had become at the tender age of twelve years.

Where had the boyish fights gone? When and where did he attain such calm and so much wisdom?

He looked no less than a concerned father figure to his brother. He soothed his little brother and at the same time comforted me.

On the way back home, I was crying silently as had become my habit since my dear husband had passed away.

Kashish had witnessed this drastic transformation in my personality. He had seen me walk through life traumatised, but had let me cope the way I wanted. He never questioned me or shared his opinion about how we must live during those challenging months.

But in the car, seeing me weeping in silence, he finally said gently, "Mumma, we are not the only ones who are facing

---

[100] *Dear brother! You nearly killed me!*

the loss of a loved one. Many people lose their partners and many children lose their fathers. Life will not stop here Mumma. We have to continue the remaining journey ourselves."

His words made me realise the worth of whatever was still left in my life.

That was the luckiest day of my life when I got my son back along with a lesson that I still had two precious jewels in my life, and have to raise and nurture them perfectly.

At the army camp, I prayed, "O Lord! My sole wish is to see both brothers together in Delhi. Please give Kashish some indication that we are safe here so that he can breathe easy. Else, he will break down. I am sure you will do this much."

Anju at this point was crying bitterly. She said, "Mausiji, do something to get Sanjay, Manoj and Anshu back. Please!"

I understood both Anju's and Neha's feelings. Their men were still stranded at the hotel. They were very tense and kept asking me to figure out some way to request the officers to rescue the three.

I got up to find the concerned officer who would heed to my request. But I saw so many other people sitting helplessly waiting for their family members. Their plight was much more miserable than ours.

The army staff was trying to console and comfort all who had been rescued and waited with baited breath to reunite with their loved ones still stranded in the flood.

I saw a lady officer trying her best to quieten a crying child of around four years. When I enquired about his mother, I was told that she had just delivered a baby and both were in a critical condition at the army hospital in the same base camp. There was no other family member to be found. The *jawans* had saved the boy, his mother and the newborn from the hospital near CH2. The boy's wailings moved everyone present there.

I asked the lady, "How is his mother? Will she be OK?"

The lady, sensing that I needed some assurance, replied, "Don't worry. She will be all right."

That little boy reminded me of my Parth. He must have cried like this when he got lost, I thought. I kept gazing at the boy affectionately and motherly feelings stirred my heart. A strong desire to pick him up and console him sprung up in me. But before I could actualise my wish, the lady got up to take him to his mother, who she said was still unconscious due to excessive bleeding at the time of delivery.

I liked that army lady for her deep, sympathetic voice and her serene face. She was holding the boy's hand gently and trying to divert his attention. She was so busy with the boy that she hardly cared for others.

Time has taught me that there is really no end to the miseries in this world. Everyone's life has an altogether different story to say. On hearing of other's experiences, we feel that our lot is so much better. The woman who had to deliver baby under those compelling circumstances, how much pain did she have to undergo both physically and emotionally?

And what about the newborn? There was very little chance of his survival. Oh, God! Please help the family. Praying was the only thing I could do for them. The incident shook me.

But for how long?

As soon as they were out of sight, they were out of my mind also. Again the eternal spirit of selfishness took over. How to get our men back? This question started haunting me.

Focus on looking out for our own group wavered only when we came face-to-face with someone's pain. But ultimately, the desire to fight for the safety of our family reasserted itself with greater force.

As only a few people had been extricated from the flood by that time, the crowd wasn't very large. But all who were there were tormented.

Some were deeply engrossed in their thoughts, some were seen rushing about in search of food, medicines, water, toothbrushes, paste, soaps, etc.

There was a small army departmental store in the vicinity. Parents with small kids were buying small packets of chips, biscuits or cold drinks. We also went to try our luck there to buy some chips and cold drinks.

Parth and Radhika stood in the long queue but before their turn could come, the store was closed as the stock of available ration had run out. We saw parents offering big amounts like Rs. 200 or more for a small-sized packet of chips, which was worth only Rs.10. Their children were desperate and were pushing them to get them some food.

But when it was announced that nothing more was available in the store, the queue slowly dissolved. The kids who didn't get anything created chaos and some of them became uncontrollable. One woman even slapped her child as he refused to understand her predicament.

Suddenly, a loud commotion was heard near by. On locating the source of the ruckus, we saw that some people were trying to tear a carton of snacks that the staff had kept safe under the table for the next lot of evacuees. More people were on their way and were supposed to reach the base camp any time with the coming boats.

The officers in charge of the foodstuff rebuffed this attempt at looting and hid the remaining stock at some inaccessible place. After that, they decided to keep strict track of all provisions.

The food stock didn't seem to be sufficient. In reality, it was not possible to arrange for so much food in such little time for such a large body of flood victims. Still, the army was doing its best.

Soon we heard some men encouraging their wives and children to go collect more food packets as no one was sure how long they would have to stick around in the unpredictable circumstances.

After mulling over this behaviour, we decided to follow suit. We wanted to keep some food for our members who were expected to reach by the coming boats if all went well. But how much time it would take was unclear.

So this became our new target and focus — go to the staff and ask for more food.

We made a plan to approach the personnel one after the other and try to gather as many consumable items as we could. We even began lying. We would go up to the distributors and say that we had not got our share. Whatever items we got, we hid them in our bags. And then again set out for another hunt.

We became no less than plunderers. No traces of decency were left in our behaviour; we were behaving like savages.

Hunger is a potent instructor. It teaches all moral and immoral means of keeping body and soul together. Honesty disappears when hunger appears.

We also abandoned all principles of civility and became obsessed with hoarding more and more. But even after so much strategic planning, we weren't artful enough to accumulate much. What we did manage were two small packets of *namakpare*[101] and one vegetable pattice. We had to be contented with our stock as it was impossible to hope for more. Even the staff had started recognising us on sight.

An officer rebuked Radhu,"I gave you something just now. Why are you turning up again and again?"

Even after that humiliation, she and Parth tried once again to add something to our pickings. But the scheme was busted and they gave up.

Having been thwarted in our attempts to hoard stuff, we turned our attention to our people stranded in CH2.

---

[101] *Deep fried savoury snack*

CHAPTER 10

9th September 2014

Around 3 p.m.

We approached the authorities to send a boat out to CH2 to rescue our group. We didn't stop after we made the first request and continued approaching them, repeating what we wanted.

What fuelled our forays was our belief that we were suffering the most and our situation was dire. Again, we lost all sense of propriety. We tried to grab the attention of every staff member so that they would relent to our demands.

We were not ready to listen to any of their explanations. Then one of them took us to the army hospital where other rescued people, who were sick and dying, were being given treatment.

He informed us that close to CH2 Hotel, there was GB Pant Children's Hospital where some pregnant women and old people were admitted. Some women had delivered their babies during the flood and now the mothers and infants were critical. The army men were rescuing them from the hospital with oxygen cylinders on. Even the infants were on small stretchers, puking in the hands of the attendants. I had seen the army rescuing newly born babies and the mothers only a few hours back.

On entering the army hospital, we panicked at the miserable sight of the patients and ceased creating any more fuss over our problem. For the first time, we realised that the army was doing its job very systematically. They were prioritising those who were most at risk.

Alas! These selfless feelings stayed only for a short while.

We are ordinary, mean-spirited mortals. Our focus was entirely on our men. Both Neha and Anju continued to run after one officer or another.

We were plagued with a dilemma…how should we ask the rescuers to send a boat to the hotel. Every single member of their team was stretched beyond endurance trying to look after the saved swarm at the camp.

But I also couldn't bear to see my nieces worried about their husbands. Who better than me would understand a husband's value?

So I got up once again to plead with an army officer to speed up the efforts. But this time, instead of something good coming off it, the situation took a turn for the worse.

I was expecting some comfort and assurance. On the contrary, he snapped and wagged his finger in my face and started screaming, *"Sirf tera hi aadmi fasaa hai? Saare log hain wahan! Ja ek side mein beth ja!"*[102]

Tears welled up in my eyes at this affront and I blurted, "Can't you speak courteously?"

He thundered, "Go away! Let us do our duty and don't interrupt."

Crying bitterly, I replied, "Don't show off your power. At least be a little polite."

By that time, many people had gathered around us out of curiosity. But nobody uttered a word against the men in command as all were in awe of them.

It had become crystal clear to everyone that only the army could help them out of this catastrophe, so all threw themselves at its mercy.

Some soldiers and a woman from the police staff came over to console me and they made me sit on a chair.

We were shattered as nothing we did was getting the desired results. With every passing boat, the hopes of seeing Sanjay, Manoj and Anshu back were getting slimmer.

We all were feeling utterly helpless. By now we had learnt one thing––we shouldn't try to create any scenes as nothing

---

[102] *You think only your man is stuck? Go, sit in a corner!*

there was possible without the army's intervention and permission.

And yet, how could we give up trying? All survival instincts were working overtime and we were all pondering over the same problem. Like a bolt of lighting, an idea hit us. Instead of any of us adults approaching the officers, we should send Aarav to plead with them!

So we made Aaru go to every soldier we could spot and instructed him to tell them weeping, *"*Mere papa ko bachao uncle, please unhe bula do.*"[103]

Aaru proved great at this. After pleading with a soldier, he would just stand around and wouldn't move.

To our sheer joy and amazement, our scheme bore fruit! The officers considered the matter seriously and finally assured us that they would send out a boat to CH2.

Whenever a boat came, a group of people would rush to see if their loved ones had finally arrived.

We wished every man coming out of the boat was our man. We were gripped with a mix of anticipation and terror. But when the men turned out to be strangers, we felt like a disintegrated body, some of whose parts had been lost on the way.

---

[103] *Uncle, please save my Dad. Bring him back to me.*

Our wait and laser focus on the incoming boats continued. Around this time, we were given vegetable pattice and a little *khichdi*[104] to eat.

What did food mean to us?

We were touching food with tears in our eyes. It was becoming impossible for us to believe that we were lucky enough to feel food on our tongues once again.

We kept our fingers crossed and continued to send Aaru to request every staff member to send a boat to the hotel. Only Aaru's words could soften the hearts of the officers. We had become totally self-focussed even though we had realised that the injured and ill must be rescued first.

We heard that more than thirty infants died due to lack of medical facilities. Their mothers and families had even stopped crying. How much could they cry?

The incident was agonizing. Still, we did not lose focus and kept up the drumbeat of getting a boat to CH2.

"Hey! Another boat has just come in! Come fast!" We dropped whatever we were doing and the same wild rushing and pushing began. All manners and etiquette of civil living fell by the wayside. Everyone wanted a glimpse of the boat and the people in it.

---

[104] *a thick gruel of rice n lentils*

207

Two members of Ujjwal's family were seen coming out of this boat––his wife and 8-year-old daughter. We welcomed them both and asked about the well being of our people.

They informed us that after saving kids and women, the army would bring in the men. This gave us some relief.

Ujjwal's family also joined our group and the excruciating ritual of waiting began again.

Time was slipping by and with the passing hours, we had turned brutal, ill mannered and terribly selfish.

We were running around like crazed animals possessed with a single desire––to catch our prey, the targets being people in charge of sending boats.

Through this endless waiting and making sorties to the authorities, we met some more influential people like the owner of a hotel in Srinagar and a team of golf players who had come to play but had gotten stuck.

They were all equally worried about their own people about whom there was no news, no updates.

Around 3:45 p.m.

One more boat arrived. We again ran with all our might. This time our eyes got a faint flash of Anshu and Sanjay. Our joy knew no bounds! We saw them stumbling towards us and we rushed to hug them and asked them about Manoj and Ujjwal. They informed us that the two were still in the queue but would definitely come soon.

We got Sanjay and Anshu's names registered in the list of the rescued people.

How we wished Manoj and Ujjwal had come too. Our hearts started sinking again. But nothing could be done. We just had to wait and watch.

The rescue operations had accelerated by then. Boats could only be sent till daylight lasted, as without lights, the rescue operation would become very dangerous.

After an hour, another boat came in. From that too, only Ujjwal stepped out.

Manoj was still stranded at the hotel.

The dam of our patience was jolted and we did not know how much longer we would be able to hold up. Neha had become nearly inconsolable and Aaru was crying without a pause.

We continued waiting and begging the officers, "Please, Sir! Only one member is missing. Please, please, please bring him back."

It was already getting dark. The approaching night would be as awful as the previous one that we had spent in the diabolic hotel.

Manoj would have to pass one more night without us in the same flooded hotel, among only a few people. We at least were safe with a whole crowd around us.

It might be very much possible that he was sitting at the frozen mouth of the tunnel since we had parted. We were dry and safe at the base camp and had replenished our empty insides with tea and snacks. But what about Manoj? He hadn't had a single drop of water, or a morsel of nourishment. Another night in that condition was beyond imagination.

Sanjay said, "We have to convince the officers somehow. If nothing is done fast, then Manoj won't be able to reach here today. And he will have to spend the night in that place again."

The thought of passing the night without him was more than enough to scare us to the core.

Sanjay somehow succeeded in making the officers understand that only a few people were left behind in the hotel and only one boat would be enough to bring them all back.

The officers heeded to his pleadings and sent the last boat of the day.

At 6 p.m.

Finally by dusk, Manoj also came bringing relief. Once again, we became one united body.

The second level of the game—The Rescue—was complete.

Manoj's name was registered in the list of rescued people.

By this time, no food was left in the camp for the new arrivals. We gave Anshu, Sanjay and Manoj eatables, which we had stocked for them. They ate some *namakpare but couldn't eat any more. We had been expecting they would devour every last bite available hungrily, but they just couldn't.

They told us that after the women and kids left, the scene at the hotel became worse than a nightmare.

Men began arguing with each other to get into the boat first. They pushed and hit each other. It was utter mayhem and the whole lot descended into savagery.

Every man was in a hurry to reach his family as time was rushing by and nightfall was closing in. Moreover, with every arrival of a boat, the chances of another one coming diminished. So everyone tried to board the one boat present. No one wanted to take a chance and wait for the next one.

Sanjay confessed that he had never heard that kind of abusive language in his life. People, desperate to save themselves, displayed their crudest side.

At one point, a bunch of young boys forcefully broke the queue and tried to board out of turn. The other locals started abusing and punching them. But the boys refused to go back to their place in the line. Instead, they tried preventing the boatmen from moving without them.

The boatmen requested them to have patience and wait for their turn. But the boys started abusing the army guys too. They adamantly refused to understand the seriousness of the situation and the need for discipline. They stubbornly said that they would go first and tried lying and making lame excuses, blind to the fact that someone could slip into the water during the tussle.

When the situation got out of hand, the locals rounded them up and gave them a sound thrashing. Seeing that, all guests stood silently at the back and let the locals be cleared first. After that incident, nobody broke the queue and moved according to their turn.

Though Sanjay wished to call Manoj when his turn came, but because of the incident, he didn't dare and only he and Anshu left CH2 together.

After they left, Manoj said that no more violence occurred and the line moved quietly. Except those boys who kept bitching about the army men insinuating that they had been deliberately left behind.

All this chaos had caused a delay in the smooth functioning of the evacuation process.

At around 6:30 p.m.

The third level of the game began.

Thousands of evacuees were sitting on the bare road of the base camp, which had become frigid. No one had any idea what was to be our next destination.

After a while, two officers arrived and asked us to form a queue to board an army bus.

In the bus, they again penned down everybody's names. The army was maintaining records of all rescued people at every step.

They were also updating this information on the Internet to communicate with affected families all over the world. The army managed the whole process impressively.

I shudder to think what trauma the families would have gone through had the army not shared the names of the rescued with the public.

We were told that since the army camp had become overcrowded, we were being sent to another safe location. They had to clear space at the base camp to accommodate more people who would arrive the next morning.

It took about half an hour to complete the needed formalities and then the bus was ready to move.

But whenever it started to inch forward, an attendant would stop it to load 2–3 more people.

The bus was already packed. But it was being stopped again and again to add more passengers. People were already sticking to one another and trying to adjust themselves in whatever little space they could squeeze into. Soon the bus was so packed that even an insect would struggle to get in!

We all stood still, immobile.

"What is it waiting for…to load MORE?????" I screamed in my head.

If it didn't move soon, I was afraid somebody would kill the driver. To no one's surprise, filth-laced abuses began to fly around.

Finally, the engine started. The driver commenced the journey to a new unknown world at a snail's pace.

But our pulse rate was galloping. It was trying to jump out of our bodies but we had to control our emotions. We were sure we would finally be on our way to dear Delhi very soon. All were sure that the ordeal was coming to an end.

The rickety, dilapidated bus, struggled along the hill shaking and jerking making us flop about like ragdolls. Fear that the bus would fall off the hill was writ large on passengers' faces.

I was sitting scared, doubting its ability to climb up that hill, especially when it was packed to more than its capacity.

Suddenly, the brakes shrieked. Some lost their balance, a few fell. "You swine! Can't you hold the rod properly?"

The bickering started and continued the whole way.

Willy-nilly it crossed the path hilly and in an hour it dropped the irritated and exhausted mob on a long and wide road.

What next?

Around 9 p.m.

The perplexed crowd stood around in the dark on a hill road in the middle of nowhere, looking for further instructions.

The hill by now was enveloped in a thick layer of fog. Out of that fog appeared a man who led us on a march up the hill. His appearance eased us a bit and we started off on a happy note almost and with some zeal. We were moving further away from the flood after all!

But the end of the road was nowhere in sight. We kept on dragging our swollen legs one step followed by another. After labouring on for at least an hour, we finally reached our destination––a temple.

Jyeshta Devi Temple. This, we were told, was supposed to be our destination for that night.

We felt we were right back to the kind of situation we had faced in CH2! It was biting cold, pitch dark and no electricity. The only difference was that we were at a higher altitude, beyond the deathly jaws of the flood.

A sizeable number of refugees like us were lying in every little corner of the temple. It was muddy and horribly cold.

We surveyed our 'camp' for the night and felt that bad luck seemed to be following us like shadow.

I suppose on a regular day, only a few pilgrims visit the temple situated in the remotest corner of the world on top of a hill. But that day it was swarming with thousands of humans. I'm sure the regular caretakers would never have imagined such a scenario.

We were advised to occupy a little space in the tent the army had pitched. That black tent was huge and a large number of people were stuffed in it like cattle.

One more batch of people was expected to reach there that night. So we hurried to grab space for ourselves inside. Surprisingly, everyone was calmly giving room to the new comers. We managed to get a little piece of ground for ourselves at the entrance of the tent.

Inside, there was no light, only extreme fright.

The moon appeared after small intervals to guide us. No sound except human whispers could be heard. Most people though were silent, engrossed in their agony. No one was able to comfort the other; they were all lost in deep thought.

Someone informed us that some food was available outside the tent. An old and desolate kitchen, whose walls looked like they would collapse on our heads if touched them even lightly, was serving a very small quantity of rice and *dal*[105].

---

[105] *lentils*

We were fortunate enough to get a little portion, though it was absolutely raw and tasteless. Nevertheless, we swallowed it somehow. At least there was something to appease our growling stomachs.

As for our throats, there was not a drop of water anywhere. It hardly mattered though. The trauma of the past few days had taught us how to exert control over our hunger and thirst.

Soon arrived the last group of the rescued, equally tired and hungry. But they reached a little late and weren't able to get even a few grains of rice.

We were sorry for ourselves but were definitely better off than the lot that came in last. We saw some of them picking up grains of rice from used plates and sharing the leftovers with their kids. But many had to sleep on an empty stomach. They did so without creating any nuisance and just kept quiet.

The bitterly cold night dragged on endlessly.

We all came back to that enormous tent as the weather outside was biting cold, penetrating right to our bones. The tent wasn't very cozy either but it was still better than being outside.

We were shivering beyond control due to our wet clothes. For the last 52-55 hours, our clothes hadn't dried.

Trying to catch some sleep, we all wished for even a 3-inch piece of shawl or blanket to cover our frozen blue feet. Two ladies took pity on us and offered to share theirs. Radhu and I, in no time, got into their blankets. Another man gave a blanket to Neha for Aarav. What kept us alive was only the heat from the next person. God only knows how our bodies had learnt to shrink themselves tight like clenched fists.

In fact, people were willingly moving into another's blanket, irrespective of gender. The most fascinating thing was that no one was making a fuss about it. The only aim was to somehow stay alive through the frosty night. Who was in the blanket——male or female——didn't matter to anyone. We all were sealed together in a box, under one roof waiting for the morning to break…hoping it would offer us better news.

We assisted each other in every way we could and were happy to be together and alive despite the hardships. We vowed not to leave the others' side under any circumstance.

But luck had abandoned us.

Because all of a sudden, that bloody rain started pouring again. It had been our continuous companion since the day we had landed in Kashmir! It seemed our woes were not yet ready to wrap up and leave.

The tent was flimsy and did not provide proper protection. From above and through all the sides, water gushed into it.

Everyone quickly got up and ran to take shelter elsewhere. We were freezing and our teeth were chattering.

Only one good thing happened––we could feel the water on our faces and opened our mouths to catch a few drops. Shivering bitterly, we were able to let raindrops coat our parched tongues with moisture. It gave us some relief.

Others also started imitating us but when the cold became totally unbearable, we rushed towards the kitchen as that was the only covered area nearby. But when we reached there, we found it jam-packed with people.

After much to and fro, we sought refuge under some broken tables that were kept in front of the kitchen to serve food to the incoming crowd. We arranged ourselves under them like a pack of cards. Water continued to seep through the cracks and the sides onto our wet bodies and shrivelled skins.

We were so drained, mentally and physically, that even in that state, we were able to fall asleep.

CHAPTER 11

10th September 2014

At around 3 a.m.

We were woken up to prepare for our next destination—— the queue to catch the army chopper to the airport.

We were still in soggy, mud-caked clothes and shivering uncontrollably. The temple was on a peak, so naturally the temperature was extremely low. I must have been less than 0 degree. Our problem was that we were drenched and that's why the cold really got to us.

And yet the temperature was not the major worry at that time. The main concern was to somehow escape from that place and reach home.

We began our journey down the hill, the same long road we had climbed up only a few hours ago. Somehow our mood improved and we began anticipating some relief finally. Our dear kids regained their spirits and tried to cheer us up on our way down.

But as soon as our destination came in sight, our hopes evaporated.

The line waiting for the chopper was so long, it seemed to have no end. It snaked for kilometres around the area.

Even the mere thought of having to stand there and wait for our turn punctured whatever hope we had mustered on our way down from the temple.

But we got in the line anyway––there was no other option. The rich and the poor were all alike––sitting on the cold road bereft of all thoughts, all hope, all faith.

I felt like a deer caught in the merciless jaw of a lion who would first rip me apart to enjoy my pain and then savour every little chunk of my flesh.

We had been knocked from one life-threatening situation to the next. At every step we would think, "If we survive this challenge, we will most definitely escape the harrowing nightmare we are in."

But the paths of struggle against every obstacle only led to the next one. And the 'next one' usually proved to be more challenging than the one before.

Contrary to normal life, we felt no need for natural calls, even to urinate, during all those days. All systems had run completely out of order. It seemed as if the organs had also understood the need of the hour and decided not to bother us.

Except for our breath, of course. It had started stinking and we were getting extremely conscious of going close one another. The foul smell from our own and other's mouths made us very uncomfortable.

Luckily, I remembered the tiny toothpaste tube I had unintentionally slipped in my pocket while fleeing from the hotel room. I squeezed miniscule amounts on everyone's fingers and told them to apply it on their teeth. All did so most eagerly. The next problem was the non-availability of water to rinse our mouths. So we just gulped the froth. Surprisingly, it gave some relief to our throats deprived of moisture for so long.

The froth that we couldn't gulp, we wiped off with our hands adding another layer of dirt on our faces which were by now already coated in layers of dust, dirt and mud, with more piling up.

After 'brushing' out teeth, we regained some confidence to talk to each other. That small tube proved to be such a blessing! It helped us resume communication. I kept it very safely in my pocket again as if it was the most valuable possession. I felt it had to be preserved with utmost care as we might need it further.

Every little thing, whatever we were left with, became a treasure for us and we could not afford to let it go waste.

During those days we understood the extreme preciousness of water, food, salt, tea, clothes, blankets, comb, oil, soap, toothbrush, paste––all things we take for granted.

Most of all, though, we realised just how valuable was a small, covered place to shelter ourselves from the harsh weather—–the rain, cold and extreme heat of the sun.

But the one thing that most people on that hillside looked for was something to put in their stomachs. Hundreds of eyes darted about to find even a tiny bit of food or a drop of water. Nobody had left any corner on that site unsearched.

We had also gone ransacking the bushes but had found nothing edible. Every centimetre looked like it had been searched clean. There was not the slightest bit of anything anywhere.

So we stood in the miles long queue without food and water. Our immediate concern was to see it move. But it didn't. Not even at a snail's pace. I wondered if it would ever?

The crowd lay scattered on every inch of the hill. It was just at the crack of dawn and it was biting cold. We prayed for warm sunrays to come out soon and protect us from the constant shivering. The hours passed by in this hope. With benumbed minds and bodies, we sat motionless on the road.

Sanjay, as usual, would not rest. I saw him moving about talking to the police and other authorities. He offered himself as a volunteer to manage the crowd.

"Where do we have to move now? What is the next step from this place? When will we reach Delhi to our loved ones?"

All these questions were plaguing the peace of his and our minds. The answer to all those questions was simple though…nobody knew!

The only thing we did know was that this 4th level would be completed on entering a giant-sized gate of the army helipad, from where choppers would transport us to Jammu & Kashmir Airport.

But was reaching the gate going to be that simple?

It was a massive iron structure with high walls all around. No one could even think of scaling the walls to the other side because the army was patrolling them. The only way in was through the gate manned by a contingent of Jammu police.

The road, right from the gate onwards, was packed. A sea of Kashmiri locals, a massive crowd of tourists and uncountable numbers of people who worked in Kashmir were present there in the hopes of getting a ride in one of the choppers.

Even millionaires waited in the same pitiable condition as us. We sat on the dirty road on which we would not even think of stepping bare foot otherwise. But in those hours, that hard road was more than welcome because at least we were on solid land away from the wrath of water.

The scary part was that the crowd was beginning to get restless. Most people had reached the limits of their endurance, which was to be expected in such horrendous circumstances when the future seemed so foggy.

It was clear God was testing the patience of every human present on the hill that morning. They had witnessed unbelievable amounts of rain, cold, hunger, thirst, destruction and even death to maintain any pretence of civility. They were fraying at the edges and slowly one or two were refusing to follow rules.

The most testing thing was a complete lack of even the slightest movement in the line. The whole crowd seemed to have frozen into a still monument, unmoving.

Only one thing brought some relief in that painfully inert hour. The sun had appeared in the sky and its warm rays began to soothe our shrivelled skin. After many days of living in frozen, wet clothes, we were thankful for the warmth slowly seeping into out bodies. For the first time in many days, our clothes began to dry.

The line, though, did not budge an inch.

I grit my teeth and wondered how much more patience was required of us?

If there had been even a little movement, I am sure everyone would have remained calm and maintained peace. After all, we all had the same motto––to remove ourselves from that hillside as soon as possible.

I can't describe how we had passed those long hours of waiting with nothing to do, to eat, or to talk even. It was just endless hours of seemingly futile waiting.

Sanjay finally decided to go figure out what the reason for the delay was. He came back soon enough, only to tell us that there was hardly any hope of getting through the gate that day.

By 10 a.m.

Within a few hours, the warmth that we had been craving for for so many days, turned unbearable. The comforting mellow sun had changed into a hot ball whose harsh rays were determined to peel off the outer layer of our skin. The scorching heat became a torment.

But, as usual, there was no escape. We had no place to seek shelter from the sweltering sun.

For some time we had been sitting on the frozen road, but in a matter of hours the ground under our butt was oven hot.

Within the span of 12 hours we had become victims of both ends of extreme weather––a freezing, wet night and now the hot, mid-day sun.

But nobody could entertain even for one moment the thought of leaving their places in the line. They had suffered too much to reach it. It was a hard-earned space and they were not ready to give it up.

As the heat intensified, so did our craving for a few drops of water. But it was such a luxury so beyond reach, we couldn't even dare to think of it. We had given in to destiny and to whatever it planned for us.

All of a sudden, we saw a large group of foreigners heading towards the gate in a separate queue. After a few minutes, the V.I.Ps and the affluent class of tourists also joined them.

We were shocked to see this favouritism. But our battered spirits had become accustomed to seeing unimaginable things happen in the last few days. We quietly watched them pass us.

While most people, like us, didn't object to a particular group being given preference, for some in the crowd it was the last straw.

Many aggressive people from the crowd got completely restless and were unable to keep their cool anymore. They were upset as all had been sitting on the bare roads since last night in such a wretched condition but had not availed anything.

A few people started throwing stones at the police. Taking a cue from them, many more joined in. The situation was rapidly descending into chaos.

On one side was the mass of rescued populace in their thousands; on the other were a handful of staff personnel, who were in charge of managing the crowd. The army was no longer manning the evacuees.

A substantial portion of the crowd was in no mood to take any more instructions and cooperate with the police.

On that hill, I could make out three kinds of groups.

First was the angry group, which was inciting others to rebel and was not in the mood to listen to any explanations given by the police. They were shouting and abusing the authorities continuously and not letting them perform their duty.

Second was the scared group, which didn't have the courage to raise their voice and was simply sitting subdued, sapped of all energy.

Last was of a bunch of volunteers comprising mainly of locals and some tourists who were continuously asking people to maintain peace and have a bit more patience.

But every attempt at controlling the restless crowd was being sabotaged by the unruly, restless lot.

The police officers urged the mob to calm down. But some people were beside themselves with rage and hardly lent ears to their words.

The number of the evacuees had also been swelling steadily, while the police force had remained small. Soon, the police stood absolutely helpless as their requests to maintain peace fell flat. If the situation wasn't going be controlled soon, it could turn into a riot.

Finally, the authorities had to take severe measures. They first tried to threaten the screamers and the rebels but were soon pushed into using their batons to silence them.

At around 12 p.m.

The sun was blazing overhead and the scorching heat became even more unbearable. We had been sitting on the road for what seemed like eternity. The same set of clothes we had been wearing for the last three days began to stink. The smell was getting too much.

We were killing time by interacting with the local people sitting next to us. They had lost every single penny and were worried about how many of their relatives had made it alive. Their plight was more than words can describe. I wondered how they would cope with the future.

Almost all were heading to Jammu as they had relatives there. Some of them had their own houses in Jammu where they spent the winter months.

I recalled most families in Kashmir worked hard to make shawls––pashmina, *toosh*[106] and other fine varieties––and kept them in bundles at home.

How light the *toosh*[107] shawls were and how exquisitely embroidered! How I had longed to purchase one with a price tag of 3 lakhs, but knew I couldn't afford it.

Those bundles were the only means of livelihood for many.

---

[106] *high-quality wool from the neck hair of the Himalayan ibex*
[107] *high-quality wool from the neck hair of the Himalayan ibex*

What had happened to those bundles? Were those marvellous shawls also destroyed in that flood? And if I was regretting so much the shawls that I had purchased and lost, then what about those weavers who had burnt the midnight oil to weave them? It usually took a year to make those high-priced pieces.

How would people console themselves over this enormous loss?

Till then I had been rueing my last purchase of pretty suits and that shawl costing 27K. But after talking to the locals, I rebuked myself.

Hunger and thirst were at their peak. A group of young boys, who were sitting beside us, went up the nearby hills, climbed some trees and plucked a few raw apples. Those apples were lemon-sized and very bitter.

We were very fortunate the boys decided to share with us their spoils. We got a small bite each. The sour juice added just a bit of life to our dead souls. Ironically, our wish for eating apples plucked off the trees was finally granted! I remembered how Hasan had refused to pluck ripe apples for us. God did fulfil our desire for fruit fresh off a tree, but how!

Seeing the boys' success, another man mustered courage and went up the hill to search for something to eat. After half an hour, he retuned as triumphantly as if he had unearthed a hidden treasure. He had found some wet, stale *chapatis*[108]. I suppose they were thrown there for the birds. But due to the continuous rainfall, the birds hadn't turned up and this man had gotten lucky.

He distributed small crumbs among his own group members. There were a couple of women in the group wearing 2-carat diamond earrings and other jewellery. There were a few children also in the group. It was very clear the group belonged to an affluent class. The kids were wearing silk *kurta pyjamas* and so were the men.

But the adversity of time doesn't spare anyone! They were also dying for small bits like all of us.

Some others tried to snatch a chapati from him but he had a firm hold on his treasure and didn't let it slip through his fingers. We also requested him to give us some, but he rudely said, "No." We sat there feeling envious of those who were relishing that stale piece of *roti*[109].

Thirst was killing me. So I began doing sheetli *pranayama*, which my yoga guru Shri SP Taneja had taught me. I recalled how during the classes he used to say that sheetli *pranayam*[110] proves to be of great help in the times of water scarcity. It produces saliva and cools the throat.

---

[108] *flatbread*

[109] *flatbread*

[110] *breath exercise*

231

It really helped me moist my dry mouth. I asked other members also to try this method but they ignored my advice.

Some people sitting nearby gave me strange looks wondering why I was making funny faces and sounds in those hard times. In fact their response made me so conscious that I gave up practising it further.

Then Parth, Anshu and Ujjwal decided to go up the hill to forage for anything edible. Some one had told them that 4-5 kms away was Chashme Shahi from where they might get some water and some thing to eat too.

The three set out on the quest for food and water to keep our flesh alive.

Anju, Neha, Radhu and I also paired up and scrounged the area to find something to eat. But with so many hungry competitors, it was out of question that we would get or even smell anything edible.

After about 2-3 hours, our three crusaders came back. With a few water bottles and two small packets of chips in their hands! The group received a hero's welcome.

What a drop of water and a few chips meant in that critical circumstance! We nibbled on little pieces only. By then, we had learnt that food was the most precious thing and it meant more than wealth.

Having something to eat and drink, we asked the boys how and where they had found this treasure. Parth said that they just followed the road we were sitting on in the direction of Chashme Shahi. For 1.5 km they went straight and saw hungry and thirsty people all along.

Then they came to a set of stone stairs going uphill. People said they would have to go up those very steep steps. They had to almost lunge up every step. This went on for a while, till they came to tarred road again. Walking again for about 2 kms, they reached the gate of an army training centre!

Many *jawans* were hanging around. The boys requested the *jawans* to let them enter as that was the only way to Chashme Shahi. Luckily, not only did the *jawans* agree to let them enter, they also came upon a shop selling water bottles and snacks! Immediately, they bought six bottles of water and some packets of chips. Only a few other evacuees seemed to have discovered the shop by then. Grateful that they didn't have to stand in another queue for food, they returned with their 'shopping'.

By the time they reached us, they had emptied a whole bottle of water and were dead tired having dragged their battered bodies up and down the hill in that heat.

As they were narrating their adventure, Anju caught a glimpse of two girls and pointing them out to me she asked, "Mausiji, aren't they the girls we met at Khyber?"

Within a fraction of a second, all three teens turned their heads to where Anju was pointing.

"Of course they are!" I exclaimed. It was Mandy and Mannat, the two girls who had so charmed us in Gulmarg.

Without missing a beat, Radhu said, "Anshu, Parth…see what has happened to your beauties. They are looking so withered."

Parth scoffed, "So are we!"

Anshu called out to them and they came over, as surprised to see us as we were to find them there.

Mannat asked us how we had reached the hill. Anshu quickly began narrating the sequence of events that landed us on the hillside.

Then it was their turn.

Mandy said, "We left Khyber on the 6th but had to face a bunch of difficulties crossing Gulmarg as the roads near the hotel were completely wrecked and clogged water made it impossible for us to drive through. After only about 4-5 Kms, our car got stuck for half a day. It took an entire day to reach Srinagar only to find the whole city under water."

Mannat burst in, "Our car was about to drown and we were close to death but we don't know how but some locals showed up and took us out of our car.

They saved us and even helped us reach the rooftop of a house that was crowded with many other helpless people. Finally, an army boat rescued us and dropped us at the army camp. We were also at the Jyeshta Devi Temple last night. In the morning we came here."

I asked, "What are you two doing here, then? Where are your parents? Why aren't you with them?"

Mannat replied, "Aunty we are looking for something to eat. Our parents are sitting in the queue near the main gate. Let me call Mumma here."

Soon their mother joined us and we exchanged notes on the calamity that had befallen us.

Parth, to lighten the sombre mood, asked, "Mandy while escaping, what did you bring along? Did you manage to save your makeup kit?"

Mandy replied, "Why and how could I do that, stupid!"

Parth clarified, "Here you have ample time. You could have tried different sorts of makeup or nail arts. Why are you wasting so much time sitting idle?"

Mock fights and rebukes followed. Frivolous banter continued which was a welcome relief and took our minds off the dire situation we were all in. After some time, we parted ways and they went back to their place in the line. We wished them luck.

The queue continued to crawl very, very slowly and more people were growing impatient. Anju and I kept walking up and down the line. But nothing seemed to be happening.

Sanjay came up with a plan. He told Anju and me, "You both go and stand near the main gate and try to cry loudly to catch the attention of the policemen. Keep at it for as long as you can. Many other women are doing the same." He said that if we got even a little lucky, they might show some mercy and let us enter the gate.

But once again, it was easier said than done.

We walked the long road and reached the main gate. The atmosphere there was very tense. The media, the police and hundreds of people were yelling and screaming at each other. Many hundreds were struggling to get in somehow. Everyone was agitated and all groups were blowing their own trumpets.

The conditions there were beyond chaotic. We took stock of the situation and realised we won't be able to create any magic there or catch anyone's attention. So we decided to go back and sit quietly in the queue.

On our way back, we saw some women who were flawlessly beautiful and unmistakably rich, wearing clothes of the latest fashion. They sat holding their heads high and with a certain poise that betrayed their wealth and pride.

We noticed their husbands were trying to impress the officers and the media, indicating that they had connections with politicians and film personalities. They were demanding that the officers let them make calls to Mumbai. But instead of requesting politely, their tone was condescending. They spoke to the authorities as if they were giving them orders.

Some officers attended to those gentlemen for a few minutes but very soon abandoned and ignored them. The men in charge neither allowed them to make a call nor listened to their tall tales.

On hearing of their men's miserably failed attempts, the women lost their cool and their poise and started screaming. They continued to name drop and speak of their contacts with higher authorities in Mumbai. Some tried to threaten the staff with a lawsuit if they didn't help. The whole matter just went from bad to worse.

We moved on. A little ahead I saw Nafisa, a Kashmiri lady who was with us in the CH2 building at the time we were stranded there.

Nafisa was a gorgeous female, with fair complexion, dark blue eyes and dark burgundy hair. She was undoubtedly attractive. She was wearing a very expensive pure *toosh*[111] shawl. Her tone was very deep and impressive, highlighting her rich upbringing.

We walked towards her and I asked, "Hey Nafisa! Finally we all meet again. What about your husband? Have you received any news of him?"

Very dejectedly she replied, "No, I still have no idea where and how he is."

---

[111] *high-quality wool from the neck hair of the Himalayan ibex*

She had already told us in CH2 that her husband had gone to Jammu on some business and he had not been able to come back due to the flood. She had to escape alone with her young daughters, one twelve and the other five.

The younger one had been crying for her father since we were in CH2. Her elder daughter continuously tried to pacify and quieten her younger sister.

She was sitting in the line alone so we asked her to come with us.

On the way, Nafisa told us that she could only bring some of her valuables but she had thankfully managed to get her daughter's school certificates. At least she could get her admitted to a school in Jammu and prevent the child from losing a year of schooling. This impressed me a lot. She valued her daughter's education more than other expensive stuff she could have escaped with.

We then saw a group of Sindhi people sitting peacefully, not creating any fuss. They were totally against the fighting and the struggling that so many were indulging in. They wanted to go according to the rules and follow the system. We overheard them saying that even if the queue moved slowly and took two days, they would not break any rules and would go as and when their turn arrived. All others sitting close to them shared the same opinion.

I was amazed at all kinds of responses from people to the same situation.

As we were walking back, there appeared a few jeeps on the road. An army major and some other high-ranking officers were in the jeep.

An angry mob stood in their way preventing further movement. Some people jumped into and some clung to all three jeeps.

They all were clamouring to get some answers to their questions, "What is the reason of the delay? Why is the police taking foreigners and others first? Why is there no arrangement of food and water even for young children?"

Though they wanted answers, they weren't letting the officers speak. Finally, the officers got in a few words explaining they were only obeying orders from higher authorities and they couldn't take any action by themselves. The drivers of the jeep had to struggle a lot to move ahead as the mob had started shouting slogans against them.

The Major was repeatedly trying to assure them that everything would be okay if they maintained peace and order.

Nafisa's elder daughter, Afroza wanted to pee so we took her to the bushes. But the bushes were badly damaged by people in search of food. And there were so many eyes peering from all sides. After much looking around, and with great difficulty, we found a suitable corner for her.

We then went back to our place. Again we sat for many hours doing nothing. The sun was blazingly fierce and we were sitting on the scalding earth without even an inch of covering over us. The intense heat was baking our heads to complete exhaustion.

Suddenly Nafisa untied her gorgeous hair to make a bun. I had never seen a beautiful shade like hers. I couldn't resist asking, "Your hair colour is very unique. What do you apply to get this shade?" She took the remark very casually and replied, "This is the magic of our famous Mumtaz *mehendi*[112] of Kashmir."

We passed two more hours this way. Nafisa was the only active one among us who kept telling her stories. She was the eldest daughter in her family and had four younger brothers. They lived in Jammu and all were financially secure.

She had bought an Innova car recently but had seen it drowning right in front of her eyes. She was scared because her husband had no idea of her whereabouts; he didn't know she had reached there alone with her daughters. But she was sure he would find them.

She was also tense about her future. How would they survive as the flood had washed away all their money? Her younger daughter, Zara, was still crying for her father. Nafisa told us that Zara was his favourite and she couldn't bear his absence.

---

[112] *organic tattoo made of henna leaves*

In those few hours there, we developed a strange sort of emotional bond with her. We were taking care of her and her daughters as if she was an inseparable part of our group.

During the whole conversation, I became emotional many times but Nafisa hardly shed any tears. This stoicism I found in almost all Kashmiris. All women were bold and strong. I observed that people from other regions—Delhi, Gujarat, Mumbai, Ludhiana, and even from foreign nations—were more restless and eager to try out ways to beat the system, legally or illegally.

But most Kashmiris had maintained a certain dignity and were dealing with this catastrophe in a calmer way. Of course, there were exceptions. Some of them behaved like us who were busy making conditions worse by flouting all rules imposed by the police.

As we did yet again after we got tired of sitting aimlessly for a couple of hours. We thought of trying out Sanjay's suggestion of going to the main gate and convincing the officers to somehow let us in. If we got lucky, they might allow us ladies and children to enter the gate. The men could follow later.

Parth asked Ujjwal and his wife also to come along but even after much persuasion Ujjwal declined our offer saying, "You people go. I'll keep siting in the queue. We'll wait for our turn to come. Only then we'll move. Anyway, if all of us go, it'll be impossible to get our place in the line back."

I asked Nafisa to come but she also said the same thing, "You go didi. Zara has just fallen asleep. If I disturb her now, she'll start crying again."

So Anju, Radhu, Neha, Aarav, I and Parth went to the main gate.

We found a large contingent of media and news reporters standing with their gadgets to interview people stranded there. But they were also not being allowed to enter the gate and meet the people inside.

The team of interviewers from NDTV approached us for our views on how the police was handling the catastrophe.

They asked us, "Don't you think politics has been playing a role here? Why is the police concerned about sending foreigners and the VIPs through the back gate while the helpless public is made to sit still without even basic necessities?"

We told them rumours were rife that Chief Minister Omar Abdullah had been trying his best to send help to the victims but due to extensive damage to Police Headquarters, Army Base Camp, Fire Brigade camps, his own offices, hospitals etc., he wasn't able to do much. He was feeling helpless on not being able to provide better rescue and relief services.

Many other people were asked the same questions to see if their views differed from ours.

Most people were of the opinion that J&K police had been trying its level best to handle the crowd but since its volume had been mushrooming up every minute so it had to surrender to people's will.

Moreover, they were indifferent to the sentiments of public and didn't seem interested in hearing out their woes. On the contrary, they were rude and apathetic.

On the whole, the entire staff had proved to be a complete failure in dealing with the devastation.

The media noted each word. They clicked pictures of the jammed road, the restless crowd, foreigners who were being cleared stealthily.

Journalist were trying their level best to enter the gate but was that so simple? They were also a part of ocean of people, all carrying the same aim anyhow to get into. They on their ends were trying to bring the plight of people into light but found themselves bound as police authority was not discriminating among any. Thus all trials simply proved futile and their entry was also resolutely restricted.

Then one of the seniors of the journalist's team offered the officers to send their tapes in which they had recorded the interviews of the stranded people inside for telecast but the staff members cleared that no arrangements could be made for the telecast as they had numerous priorities than telecasting their tapes. Such a multitude was standing starving and shattered and they did not justify to spend even a single second on any other sort of plea. So the media also stood dejected but baffled up for not been able to provide assistance to the crowd.

Our group, along with many other women, pushed our way to the front and requested the police to let us enter. Everyone was weeping. Some even fell at the officers' feet and begged to be allowed to enter. All had different reasons for wanting to get ahead before others in the line.

Some said their babies were falling sick. One man said his father was old and was a heart patient and couldn't endure such conditions.

Then another man said, "Sir, my wife has started menstruating and she is bleeding a lot. She needs some sanitary pads urgently. Please, please allow her to go in." He was standing behind his wife trying to hide her modesty and soiled clothes but he hardly could! People were pushing and shoving others so savagely.

It was strange that police had become indifferent to all these emergencies. But one among them, who appeared very stern, pitied the woman and allowed her to get in.

While she was wriggling her way in, we pushed hard so we could also get in. In this effort, Parth's knee was hit by somebody's suitcase and he winced in pain. He caught my hand, almost digging his fingers into my flesh and cried out loud. Anshu took him aside and made him sit in a corner. My eyes kept searching for him. Suddenly, the same policeman allowed all women of our group and Aaru inside the gate.

In a flash we went through and the gate was slammed shut behind us. No male member was allowed to come inside.

I turned around to see the world from which I had just escaped. My soul, mind and body started trembling with fear. I saw my Parth and all others terror stricken, their faces distorted with desperation. They were pleading with the officers at the gate and the officers were pushing them back forcefully with all their might.

Tears roll down my cheeks, when I recall those moments in which people were treated worse than animals.

We saw a young man of around 24-26 years, in front of the main gate, screaming at the police. In a fit of rage, he rushed forward but was beaten back by police sticks. His wife ran towards him to pull him up and begged him to stay quiet. They seemed to be a newly married couple as the woman was wearing a bright pink suit and the auspicious *churra*[113], the red bangle set which is a symbol of a newly wedded Punjabi bride.

The situation was fast deteriorating. Even recalling those incidents of desperation, rage and utter chaos all around still brings sweat on my forehead.

I craved to disappear in a small, dark corner where I could cry out aloud. Such a horrible tragedy!!

---

[113] *a red and white bangle set newly wedded brides wear*

"Oh God! Are you there? Why have you abandoned us?" my heart cried.

I had listened to my parents' tales of India–Pakistan partition; of how they had to run empty handed for their lives leaving all possessions behind.

Our struggles in Kashmir reminded me of that. Had it been as difficult as this for them? Or had it been worse?

Thinking of my parents opened the floodgates of repressed grief. I was inundated with images of my late parents, my mother-in-law and my husband who had all been with me some years back. How lovely life was at that time!

"Where have they all disappeared?" I cried in absolute despair.

I just spiralled down an emotional rabbit hole. "Oh, God! Is there nobody in this world who can embrace me at this wretched time and comfort me."

I just wanted to hear my husband's words––"Don't worry about anything, Renu. *Main hoon na!*[114] I will do everything needed. You just relax."

But there appeared nobody,
Actually, there is nobody.

---

[114] *I am here*

So far, I have been managing all challenges by myself so that I can raise my kids well. I have been able to plan and play my part successfully and that is because all three of us are together. I feel blessed I have nurtured two sons who have cried and smiled with me through all the taxing moments of life. And we have settled nicely in our respective careers.

"But today, what has brought us here? Have we not gone through our punishments yet? Is there still a long road of woes ahead of us?"

It was the second time we had been parted from our group members. The pain I had felt when we moved away from the hotel in the boat without our men gripped me again. We were once again leaving them behind to struggle alone in the quagmire of uncertainty and despair.

Sensing every minute pass slowly, I felt pangs of panic stirring inside me. What would we do if the authorities didn't let our men in?

The approaching night added to our worry. We found it hard to carry that burden. So we gathered whatever little courage was left and went back to policemen.

By now, we had mastered the art of pleading with the authorities. So, we formed four groups and one by one we went and requested the staff manning the gate to permit our men to come inside.

After many attempts, the policemen allowed us to identify our people. We pointed at them. We tried looking for

Ujjwal, his wife, Nafisa and her daughters but we couldn't find them in the crowd pressed against the gate.

One after the other, our family members were allowed to enter and the gate was shut. While they crossed, abuses were hurled at us. People objected, pushed, pulled clothes and hit.

As the men came through, we welcomed them with teary eyes. At the very outset I asked Parth, "How is your knee?" Just to avoid worrying me, he pretended to be brave enough to endure the pain and didn't show any traces of suffering. But I knew he was not okay so I held him to me.

Once again we all were together and that joy was more than becoming a billionaire overnight.

The 4th level was accomplished.

At 7 p.m.

With some cheer, we proceeded to look at the new place we had arrived at. It was the army helipad, a vast open area surrounded by small hills.

Our joy deflated within seconds. A humongous crowd lay scattered all around. The number of people at the helipad made our heads spin.

All our dreams of soon going home came crashing down.

Our faces turned pale, we stood lifeless like corpses. No one felt like uttering a word. Anyway, we contained our disappointment and wore hollow smiles.

We realised we were looking at our next challenge. A new target stood before us.

The only way to move further was to board one of the choppers to the Jammu Army Airport. But how to catch one when countless other people had the same target?

With every level, the challenges we faced got harder and harder. Willingly or unwillingly, we had to accept them.

The immediate problem was how to pass that bitterly cold night in that open area. It was freezing and there was no light, water, food, connectivity, or washrooms. Tall trees surrounded the whole area. They would have looked beautiful in happier times, but that night they seemed like growling ghosts with satanic shapes.

There was something ominous about the place. An intangible fear permeated the entire atmosphere. We were not convinced we would get undisturbed sleep even though we were in an army camp. We felt unsafe.

An unreasonable fear took hold of me that at midnight someone might dig a dagger in our hearts and the soldiers meant for our safety would fail to protect us.

Nevertheless, we hunted for a decent place to sit and luckily got shelter in the veranda of the lone office building in the area.

The veranda had a cemented roof but was open on three sides. It was not enough for all of us and only a few managed to sit there.

My ankle was still aching severely and I was dying for a painkiller. I realised how worthy even one small tablet is. We had enough money and were wearing gold and diamond ornaments. Yet, all I craved for was a small pill.

Money makes a mare go. We have heard this proverb many times and it has proven its worthiness in most cases. In our dear Delhi, the power of money and contacts generally helps resolve all problems easily.

There is hardly any room for honest dealings there.

Gone is the era when the scales of justice were prompt and genuine. Now, every task can easily be accomplished by greasing the palms of people in the chair.

We have begun finding this system of working very comfortable and honestly we don't mind it at all as we have become accustomed to it. In some ways, it makes the lives of people with money easier. Jiggle some coins if you've jumped a red light, haven't secured admission in a school or college, or wish to get a government job. Any sort of hindrance and money can make it disappear.

But not at the army helipad. Money had no meaning during the devastation. Gold had lost its glitter.

We had almost 5 to 6 lacs of rupees in cash with us, and several credits cards. And the jewellery, which we were wearing, must have been worth around 40-50 lacs. We were ready to part with all if anyone could get us out of this place.

But no body was desirous of our money. No one and no amount of money could get us out of this hell. Nothing but the sharpness and alertness of our minds could produce some magic and save us from that place, if God so wished.

At 8 p.m.

In that limited space in the veranda, six of us got shelter. Anshu, Parth and Sanjay lay on the frosty helipad ground that was amazingly cold.

Things worsened when Neha's trouser belt loop got entangled with a sharp object in the wooden pillar she was leaning against. When she tried to get up, it tore, not just the loop but the trouser as well.

She cried aloud and turned her back against the wall. She was hugely embarrassed.

We comforted her, "Don't worry Neha, it could happen to anybody. We'll do something."

Anju went and explained the whole matter to Sanjay and Anshu. Sanjay told Anshu to give his pants to Neha. Though it was not an easy decision to strip off one's clothes in the chilly night but Anshu, realising his moral obligation, took off his trousers and willingly gave them to Neha.

The next question was, how she would change since we were in open grounds teeming with people. We wrapped Anju's shawl around Neha and somehow she changed trousers right there.

Though Neha was comfortable after this, Anshu only had a pair of boxers to protect him from the freezing night. He sportingly went out in open, but soon turned blue due to excessive cold. We gave him the shawl to wear as a *lungi*[115] for some warmth.

On seeing him dressed that way, some boys who had just arrived passed sarcastic remarks. "Kya baat hai bhai! Ready for a ramp walk even in this condition. That's called spirit. How about showing us some of your moves?" they taunted.

Anshu lost his head and told Parth, "Come, lets go show them some moves and let our hands talk to them." But Parth and others convinced him the fight wasn't worth it.

We had taught our bodies and minds, which were nearly ready to revolt, to ignore most of the hardships that seemed to have no end.

No body had been to the washrooms for the last three days and still we felt no urge. You know, the naked truth of life

---

[115] *cloth tied around waist extending to the ankles*

is that when a bigger sorrow appears, the little ones capsize. Similarly, the need for basic necessities had receded as we fought to keep ourselves alive.

I lay there and wondered about the irony of our being at the helipad. In this highly protected and restricted army zone, where no civilian can dare to step in, we walked about as if it was a common bazar.

The situation would have been entirely different if we had come to visit as normal visitors on the recommendation of some highly influential person. Then we would have considered ourselves the luckiest people who had somehow gained permission to visit a restricted zone. We would have narrated stories of our tour to our near and dear ones, spicing and embellishing them as usual.

But we had reached there without anybody's recommendation and so we did not value it at all. In fact, we couldn't wait to get out of the place.

The earth below us was no less than an ice sheet and we were forced to lie there without any blankets––neither to spread under our bodies nor to cover ourselves. My Parth, who can't pass winter nights in Delhi without nasal drops as he catches cold very frequently, seemed to be breathing normally.

I really felt like hugging my sweetheart for being so uncomplaining. But I didn't do anything. We were so drained, physically and emotionally, that we had no energy left for anything but saving our precious lives.

Sanjay as usual was roaming about in the search of some way to better the situation. He approached the officers to ask them if they could provide us blankets or any covered area somewhere inside the buildings and offices.

When all his attempts failed and he was sure nothing more could be done, he settled on the cold hard ground on the helipad to wait for dawn. But soon he came to us shivering and we spared a bit of place for him on the veranda.

Though we wanted to adjust Parth and Anshu also with us, other people started shouting, "You requested place for one person and we adjusted. Now you want to call two more?"

One of them even threatened to throw all of us out of the veranda if we didn't mend our ways. Sanjay, sensing their anger, spoke to them politely, "*Bhaiya* cool down, nobody else is coming. Let's maintain peace."

We didn't argue and let Anshu and Parth sleep on the helipad.

I was racked with guilt. The motherly love I showered on Parth in our house––spreading quilts or extra sheets for him at midnights in wintry seasons––was nowhere to be seen. How could a person let their identity alter in such a short span of time?

I let him sleep on the icy-sheet of a ground, while I slept under the protection of a roof at least. To my extreme amazement, I felt as if I, all of a sudden, had become his daughter and he in every sense was showing fatherly concern for me.

The roles had reversed. Throughout this ordeal, he had been worried about my safety every second. He was concerned about my pain only and never spoke of his own. He always tried that I shouldn't suffer any more than necessary.

My little boy always grumbled at home and made endless demands——"I cannot lift so much baggage and climb stairs. Our house should be on the ground floor." That boy had transformed overnight. He ensured I did not pick any heavy luggage and took care of every single member of the group.

Time is a great teacher.

We had made desperate efforts to reach where we were and our kids had exhibited exemplary courage throughout. Nobody cribbed about anything. They had matured a lot in those 3–4 days. All three teenagers had been transformed into adults.

Anshu, who was known for his funny and immature ways, who always obsessed about brands, watches, cars and hotels was also contributing his bit and helping everyone out. Radhu, our tiny princess, whose existence revolved around applying nail paints, chatting on phone, watching TV and fretting and fuming if asked to lend a helping hand with chores, had also changed. She kept trying to lessen the stress levels all around. She also took charge of the bag in which her mother's money and precious things were stored.

I noticed many times that even while dozing, she never let her grip on it loosen.

And Aaru too was a blessing. Ceaselessly, in the midst of all the danger, he kept up his naughty ways.

He would suddenly hold Parth and bombard him with kisses saying, "I love you Parth *bhaiya* because your face is so cute."

Parth would shoo him away with threats of a thrashing if he didn't behave. Aaru, giggling naughtily, would run away only to repeat the same ritual just as soon as Parth relaxed his vigil against the little one's never-ending ambushes.

Aarav's antics and his spirit had constantly taken our minds off the immediate emergency and provided us relief from ceaseless stress.

The best thing about him was that he never made any unreasonable demands. He was happy with his 'survival kit' and his measly goodies in it, which we all had vowed not to touch no matter how hungry we got.

CHAPTER 12

11th September 2014

2 a.m.

We had not been able to settle into sleep properly, when a loud quarrel nearby woke us. We rushed out of the veranda and looked around. A large group of around 300-400 local people, which included Muslims, *Pandits*, and local Punjabis, had gathered at the helipad and were screaming and shouting.

Those people were part of the long queue on the helipad. They had come a day before us, perhaps on 9th September, and were being evacuated by choppers according to their turns.

The system had been running smoothly till we heard the noise. We asked people around us what had happened but no one had any clue.

On listening intently for a while, we were able to discern what the commotion was about.

The majority of the agitated crowd was demanding that they get to take the choppers first. Being employees in various government departments in the state, they had served the Government for years. Tourists, on the other hand, were outsiders and had come to their land only for a few days. On account of being natives, they argued, they deserved to be saved before the temporary visitors.

The men on duty tried to pacify the infuriated crowd but failed miserably. People were so riled up, they had become adamant and all pleas fell on deaf ears. They threatened to disrupt and derail the whole operation if their demands weren't met.

I suspect the group had sensed that stopping them was beyond the capabilities of the limited police personnel. And they weren't wrong in their assessment. The handful of helpless staff members stood around like mute spectators.

Watching this drama unfold so close to me, I felt I was witnessing before my very eyes the mob violence in Kashmir that we keep hearing and reading about regularly on TV and newspapers.

For the first time I realised the difference between watching an angry mob on TV and actually being so near one that its rage becomes palpable.

A flood of experiences, unthinkable in a normal life, had been unleashed on us on this trip. And the torrent seemed in no mood to abate just yet. We had been bombarded with so many 'first-time-shocks', we had lost our bearings and were in a compete daze. Looking at the swelling mob, I wondered how many more shocks were yet to come.

But generally what happens with a calamity is that

When we hear, we fear
When forced, we bear….

On that black, gloomy and frozen night, we stood helpless watching the unbelievable tableau unfold and a strange fear gripped us.

We were still reeling from the impact of the flood and trying to grapple with what it all meant, when we found ourselves witnessing a strife with regional and religious undertones.

All Kashmiris in white *kurta pyjamas* demanded in unison, "We are employees in different offices in the state and have served the valley for years. We deserve every right to be despatched before others so we only will go first." They kept repeating the same sentence over and over again.

Some officers tried to pacify them but some of them very adamantly reasoned," Sir, suppose fire breaks out in your area then will you save your family first or let the whole crowd of the area be cleared and after that you will think of your evacuating your own family"

The same is the case with us. Till the time, we, the original inhabitants are not sent we will not let tourists go even.

To some extent their demands didn't seem illogical. After all they were also common humans who prioritized their families as we had.

So the staff stopped taking any initiative to intervene and calm the crowd. They simply stood around quite sure that the matter was beyond their capabilities to handle. So, they did not even try.

But some aggressive tourists got annoyed at these unreasonable demands. After all, they had also been waiting in the same queue for as long as the locals.

This group of tourists tried to challenge and oppose the demand and began to argue with the sloganeering crowd. Heated arguments flared up and it soon devolved into a bitter quarrel.

The tourists said that everybody should go as per turns. If the Kashmiri group was allowed to go first, then they would not keep mum and fight for their rights. They said that since they were guests in the state, it was the duty of the government to ensure their safety first.

Both parties, like clever lawyers, threw arguments at the other group to prove that their logic was better than the others. The decibel levels soon reached a point where no one could hear anything clearly, though the local group was definitely more aggressive. All of a sudden, someone from that group took out a gun and fired a shot in the air.

The whole crowd shuddered with fear at the suddenness of the bang. After a fraction of a second's stunned silence, everyone started rushing away from the nuclei of the crowd, trying to hide in whatever corner they could.

Earlier, everyone was shivering of cold, now they shivered with fear of death. People had run to this helipad to escape death, but the spectre of death seemed to have followed them.

We were beyond shocked to see this surreal turn of events. Such extreme outrage was beyond belief.

The tourist group that had been so vociferously putting up a fight till then melted away like a lump of sugar in the mouth. After that gunshot, not one of them uttered a single word and simply gave in, submitting to their uncertain destiny. Not just the people participating in that argument, but everyone in that open ground ran in one direction— towards the hanger.

The hanger was the only covered area where we could get shelter. It was empty, as all choppers usually parked there had been deployed to pick and drop passengers.

That place would easily keep us out of the reach of that angry gang. The whole mass stuffed itself into that vast space which now seemed too small for all those wanting to get in.

People were terrified of going out and facing that livid mob.

The gap between rich and the poor; able and disabled; boy and girl; Delhi and Punjab had been washed away and equality established with one press of the trigger. People quietly let others squish against them without any inhibitions.

All sat like a herd of meek and mute animals at the mercy of the Lord. Only if He wanted they would move.

We had lost all hope and passed those hours in terrible suffocation as our sense of despair deepened.

The victims of nature were now polarised...one big group was on the helipad and the other in the hanger.

It was like a huge swarm of buzzing bees inside the hanger. Everybody was murmuring but nothing was clearly audible. In our heart of hearts we knew that our turn would come only after that volatile group outside was cleared first. But with so many of them, it was highly doubtful the task would be accomplished any time soon.

Every inch of army grounds––the helipad, its gardens, the hanger, and every bit of the land available was occupied with people waiting to be airlifted.

I don't know whether I have ever encountered so many people all at once. Even if I strain my mind hard and try recalling every crowd I have seen in the past, I don't think I have come across such an ocean of humans––not at saintly discourses, not at political rallies and not even on the silver screen.

Who could airlift this multitude from there? Would it even be possible? In those terrible hours, the mission seemed next to impossible.

Trying to take my mind off the despair, I looked around and discerned three different kinds of people trapped in that vast area.

The available officers were trying to keep order as best as they could with their limited numbers. All links––telephones, roads, railways were severed and trying to function in such a paralysed state, the police was failing spectacularly.

Then there was the large group of angry locals scattered over the helipad and ready to kill whosoever dared to enter the gate.

The remaining group was the hopeless and unfortunate pile of people, the 'outsiders' who had submitted to whatever fate had in store for them.

Our problems were multiplying rather than getting resolved. At that point, the four levels of the game of survival that had already been crossed seemed much easier than this one.

We felt horribly hooked and kept wondering how we were going to escape this prison.

The rest of the dreadful night passed in listening to the threatening slogans of the locals––both Muslims and *Pandits*. They had united themselves into a single body for this particular cause, though retaining their separate identities like the yolk and white of an egg. That body was determined to get its demand carried out.

Things would have deteriorated if anyone had intervened, giving rise to bloodshed and violence. So neither the police nor the tourists tried to stop them. The police simply roamed around the area and our helpless group stayed put in the hanger.

The night dragged on.

At 9 a.m.

Though the impressions of the previous night were still vivid in our memory, some people went out to have a look at the helipad on hearing the noise of the choppers. The mob of the previous night was still persistent but the numbers had somewhat reduced.

Only a few choppers were landing and that too not too frequently. They took out only the VIPs, the foreigners and a few people of that maddened crowd. The same procedure continued till noon.

Inside the hanger, it was becoming unbearable as there was nothing to do, nothing to talk about, nothing to eat, nothing to drink. Moreover, nobody was able to lie down properly. For how many hours could a person sit idle?

Gradually men started going out of the hanger to check on the latest proceedings. But everybody maintained a safe distance from the queue after the night's incident.

Around two hours later, Anju, Anshu, Parth and I also stepped out to breathe some fresh air. While wandering around, we came to the area near the main gate. We saw the same big crowd struggling desperately to enter. They were shouting, crying, begging to be let in!

I wished I could tell them that the situation on this side of the gate was more pathetic than outside. They were unnecessarily exerting themselves to get in, like we had a day before. I wished to tell them that there was absolutely no guarantee of reaching the airport even after all the effort. But I didn't. I just watched them in mute silence.

After a while I noticed 15-20 tourists, who had been fighting with the local group at night, trying to go out from the main gate with their baggage.

I couldn't stop myself from asking them, "Why are you going out? You got in with such great difficulty! How can you even think of getting out of this place?"

They replied, "Nothing will happen by just sitting around here. The police is completely incapable of evacuating so many people. We've heard that there is another road route out of this place from Chashme Shahi. Though we will have to walk for a few miles to get there, we can at least hire a jeep there to drop us to Srinagar Airport. So we're going to try our luck there."

One lady, utterly dejected, mumbled, "We have been in the queue for one and a half days and when our turn came, the other group created this nuisance. I feel we'll all die, either here or there! We are going to a better place to die."

That was the height of their disappointment.

But the conversation made me think we could also try the same route. Actually, we were also convinced that nothing was possible there so we rushed to Sanjay excitedly to inform him of the newly discovered route.

We shared with him what the group swimming against the tide had told us. In fact, around 50-60 more people had joined them enthusiastically. After days of inertia and despair, they looked excited about having found a way out. They were strongly recommending others to follow them as it was a mere waste of time and energy sitting there on the helipad.

"Whenever your turn comes, you'll face the same fate as ours. There is no law and order here. Let's get out of this hell."

There was such conviction in their words that we too were swayed and pressurised Sanjay to follow suit.

But Sanjay?

As always, he refused to listen to others' fantasies and followed his own logic. He strictly forbade us to lend ears to the 'nonsensical' tales.

But we kept insisting that we could at least try. Before our very eyes more than a hundred people had gone out of the gate and the number was increasing.

Sanjay rebuked, "Have you all gone mad? Have you forgotten the struggle we faced to get in? Are those people who are still dying to come inside stupid? If there is any other route, then why are people sitting outside not running for it?

Listen to me. We are not going anywhere and will stay here until a chopper takes us."

Chastised, we silently walked away towards the helipad. But a huge rush of people was heading for the gate. Again we pleaded, "Sanjay, at least talk to them! Isn't it possible they might be right."

Exasperated, Sanjay turned to Parth and Anshu, "You both went to Chashme Shahi yesterday. Did you hear anything about this route?"

"No, we didn't," replied both in unison.

But the temptation to follow the mob was too strong. We kept coming up with reasons why we should follow the herd.

Constant pressure from us, and the swelling throng headed for the gate chipped away at his resolve and he finally talked to them.

Their enthusiasm and absolute conviction influenced him a bit and he agreed to trying something other than just waiting, but on one condition. Only Anshu, Parth and he would go out to see whether the new route was a rumour or there was any truth in it. We readily agreed with him and let the three of them go take a look.

Sanjay approached the guards on the duty to allow them to go out. He told them that one of our members was missing and they wanted to look around for him. He promised they would come back in an hour. This way he kept both options open and tried ensuring a hassle free exit and return if needed.

We saw them go out and commenced yet another cycle of waiting.

We had hardly been waiting for five minutes when we heard a woman wailing. I turned my head around and found Nafisa crying inconsolably. Anju and I ran to her and asked, "Nafisa! What happened dear? Why are you crying?"

Nafisa could barely manage to reply, "Didi, Zara… Zara"

"Zara! What happened to her? Where is she?" my heart skipped a beat.

"I don't know *'Di*, I can't find her anywhere. While getting in through the gate, she got lost. I thought Afroza was holding her hand but on reaching inside we found her missing. I don't know what to do now?" Nafisa sobbed.

I felt a stab of pain in my chest and my eyes filled with tears. I found myself awash with the same sense of panic I had felt when my 6-year-old Parth had gone missing.

Anju and I tried our best to console her and promised we would find her daughter. Nafisa was beside herself with grief. Afroza also started crying.

We took them to an officer and requested him to do something to find Zara. After repeated announcements, some guards brought a girl inside. They said that they had spotted her standing outside the gate crying. When they asked her name, she told them that she was Zara and had lost her mother and sister.

Thankfully she was found! Zara, on recognizing her mother, threw herself in her arms.

Nafisa sobbingly asked, "Where were you Zara my *jaan*?[116] Your *ammi*[117] almost died."

Zara blubbered that she had mistaken some other girl for Afroza and followed her to the gate. But it was already closed and she couldn't see her mother or sister anywhere.

Nafisa put the scared girl in her lap and soothed her. When they all settled a bit, I asked Nafisa, "When did you come inside and where is Ujjwal and his family? Weren't they with you?

Nafisa recounted, "After you entered last evening, the gate was closed and the rest of the crowd had to spend the night on that chilly road. We remained with Ujjwal's family.

The night was pitch dark, cold and scary. But all seemed OK until an incident of eve teasing. Some boys cracked vulgar

---

[116] *darling*
[117] *mother*

jokes about girls sitting nearby and taking advantage of the darkness, tried to touch them immodestly.

The girls screamed and their parents beat the boys black and blue. Some others joined in and threw those boys out of the queue.

It frightened us and we made all three girls sit in the middle of the group. We warned the girls not to move about without us.

An hour passed peacefully before another family was heard crying in distress.

It was a local family of meagre means who had packed all their wealth––cash, jewellery etc.––in a bag while evacuating. That bag was their only means of starting life afresh.

Somebody had stolen it under the cover of darkness. Now they were ruined completely."

Their cries, she recalled, were heart-rending.

She continued, "People tried looking for the thieves but to no avail. Everyone in the crowd immediately became more vigilant. In fact, a few men took it upon themselves to patrol the place from one end to the other end of the line. They walked about the entire night to ensure that no such incident happened again. Soon enough, they spotted 2-3 goons trying to lay their hands on others' possessions. They caught them red-handed and handed them to police."

She recounted how they spent a harrowing night outside the gate.

"In the morning, the same struggle for the entry to the helipad started again. There was no discipline and no system; getting through depended solely on the might and ingenuity of a person."

She said the police refused to open the gate at all saying, "The helipad is already overcrowded. No more people can be accommodated. When some from inside are cleared, only then we'll let a fresh lot in."

But when the gate opened slightly for those going out from there, people standing outside pushed and got in.

"We were with Ujjwal's family till then but while struggling to enter, we lost each other. I somehow managed to get in only to realise Zara was missing," she concluded.

She now asked us, "*Di*, why are these people going out from here?"

I narrated to her the whole tale of the previous night and their reasons for leaving the place. I also told her that Sanjay and our sons had also gone out to see if there was really another way out.

She was very surprised and said that nobody from outside knew of any such route, else they would've also tried.

On hearing her words, our confidence they would find an alternate route was punctured, but we still sat with our eyes glued to the gate hoping every moment that the men will return with good news.

At 3 p.m.

We had a glimpse of our men pleading with the guards to let them in and the guards denying them entry again and again. Anju and I ran and told the guards, "They are our people. Please, Sir! Let them come in."

The guards growled, "This is the last time we are allowing you. Don't try any tricks again."

The men entered…with red, angry faces!

Sanjay, as soon as he kept his foot inside hissed, "Happy now? You know how much we had to walk just to find out if there was anything in a silly rumour? There is no such way out! People are simply building castles in the air."

Parth panting, grunted, "Please don't fall prey to such nonsense and use your minds. Lets sit here and wait for our turn no matter how many hours or days it takes."

Anju and I shamefacedly tried to avoid their angry eyes and slowly disappeared from the spot and came to the helipad.

We saw choppers landing, though not very frequently. But one thing was astonishing——the tense and angry crowd of locals was thinning from the helipad. Their numbers were reducing with every hour thus lessening the chaos.

It was very much possible the authorities had understood that if they had to maintain harmony, then angry locals had to be cleared first. Else, they wouldn't let anybody go.

Around 4 p.m.

Sanjay spotted a man talking to someone on his phone. Stunned at the sight, he asked the man, "How did you charge your battery?" But the man didn't answer and went away.

Sanjay was still wondering how the man was talking on phone, when all of a sudden he saw a flickering bulb in the hanger. It occurred to him that perhaps power had been restored. He immediately rushed to the hanger and started ransacking every single inch of the place to find a charging point. After much effort, he did manage to find one!

He quickly plugged in his mobile to recharge the battery but realised the supply was low. Almost after an hour, it had charged only 10%.

It was no small achievement. Out of the crowd of thousands or more, he must have been only the second or the third person to use his presence of mind to restore connectivity. The rest of us were caught up with petty and obvious things like where to sit, the sun, the cold, and our number in the queue.

Sanjay was overjoyed and immediately tried to make a call to his father but unfortunately the call couldn't connect. Then he sent him an SMS, "We are safe and have reached the army helipad. Inform others."

But the SMS also failed to be delivered.

He didn't give up hope and tried to catch the signal to somehow get the message delivered. He had found yet another goal and got busy in reaching it. He carried around the mobile to different locations, holding it up high in his hands to catch the signal and send his message.

In the meanwhile, the rest of us hung around the helipad to keep a tab on the process of evacuation.

One by one, people boarded the choppers and the mass of humanity began to shrink and by late evening the entire group of locals had vanished. The helipad was once again at the disposal of the tourists and others.

The spring of hope sprang up again
All hoped to board the next plane.

But nothing had been easy till then. The pattern continued.

It had already started getting dark and the biting chill was fast spreading like fire in a hearth.

Soon, the arrival of choppers stopped and rescue operations resuming that night was out of question. Whatever had to happen would happen only on the following day.

Yet again, we were face to face with the terrible problem of how to pass the night?

The soul shaking experiences of previous nights struck terror in our hearts. Even the thought of sleeping in the open on bare land again was frightening.

Suddenly, Sanjay came beaming triumphantly that his SMS was finally delivered. We were relieved that at least our families would heave a sigh of relief knowing we had survived.

He immediately jumped to the next challenge, "Hurry up to grab some space in the hanger as electricity has been restored. Everybody is rushing in to get hold of the charging points."

But we were not only the intelligent ones we realised.

Almost the entire hanger was already full, but somehow Manoj had managed to get some space and settled comfortably.

In fact, Manoj had proved yet again that no one was better than him at finding a place in the queue or in a crowd. Right from the beginning of the mishap, this had been his sole focus and duty.

Seeing him, Neha, Aaru and Radhu proceeded towards him. They had to face harsh words from people who had stretched their legs as far as they could to occupy maximum space so that they could sleep properly at night. There was no alternative but to ignore their words.

One by one, the three merged and settled into the crowd. Parth and Anshu went out to find space in the veranda. Sanjay, Anju and I tried our luck on the helipad. But we didn't find even a patch of land unoccupied on it.

This time I noticed with shock that the crowd had doubled! Since last night we had been praying, "O! Lord, let hot-headed locals be cleared fast so that we might finally get a chance to leave." But suddenly, there stood a crowd almost double the size compared to the previous night.

How could this be?

We came to know that the evacuation and rescue process in the valley was speeding up and more and more people were being dumped in the area, for the next stage of evacuation. Hence, a huge number had been let in from the gate.

On seeing this sea of people, Sanjay approached the army officers to confirm that we would be dispatched the following day. Sanjay, the iron man of our group, also burst into tears and begged for our exit. The officer in charge promised him that he would do his best. We had hardly any faith in the officer's promise but pretended that we truly trusted him.

At 8 p.m.

A bunch of personnel ordered the crowd, "Make a queue and sit silently if you want to get something to eat."

They promised that if the crowd cooperated, all would be given *pooris* to eat. Almost everyone was in the death-grip of hunger and thirst. And the word *poori* fanned the flame further.

We began recalling the taste of wheat on our tongues; we began dreaming of touching luscious *pooris* with our fingers.

Without any further enquiries or questions, the hopeful mob morphed into a queue. The cacophony on the helipad died out. It became very quite with everyone plonked on the freezing ground in a line like nursery class children. There was almost pin drop silence and we could feel the eagerness in that waiting crowd.

Some men came with bananas and started serving us one each. When we got the fruit in our hands, we devoured it in seconds. We kept chewing on the peels too, which had never before seemed edible. I almost ate half of it without realising I was eating something I normally throw away. Then I decided to eat the rest of it anyway. How could I have thrown anything that could be eaten? Especially something which we had acquired almost after 40 hrs of hunger!

Oh, God! What relief!

But then our intestines, which had been hibernating for so many days, suddenly woke up and started demanding more. We kept our fingers crossed for the *pooris*.

No body turned up with them for quite a while. But the aroma indicated that they were on their way and so we did not move from that place. The hope that it would be coming soon or say after 10–15 or 30 minutes kept us glued to the cold, bare ground. Not a single soul dared to shift even a bit or make any noise.

But when people sensed that the promise might have been a ploy to fool the aggressive crowd so it could be quietened, some from the line got up to ask the reason for delay in the distribution of the *pooris.

To their astonishment, they were thoroughly scolded by the officers who complained, "You people are not cooperating so we're serving them in the hanger first."

That triggered a rat race to the hanger. Anju and I also got up to see what was happening. On reaching inside we were informed that some *pooris were supplied to every family, and Manoj and others had also got 2-3 *pooris.

We divided them amongst ourselves and everyone managed to get a few bites. Though it was terribly hard and burnt, I would never be able to pen down the taste and the satisfaction it provided us.

A few families were not lucky enough to get any and their children started crying. Some threw tantrums and their parents were not able to reason with them. I saw a woman begging for a *poori for her crying daughter from her neighbours but everybody had become so selfish that even on seeing the little baby crying, nobody shared anything.

We had also become so greedy that we turned our heads in the other direction when our eyes met with those of the hungry children, all the time fearing for the safety of our share. We also wanted to eat more as we were starving and our unsatisfied stomachs were rebelling against co-operating any more.

We approached the staff to ask for more. They told us that they had already distributed everything they had. They further added that the staff members themselves had been working on empty stomachs for the last 2 days. Only a few bananas were left for them.

They said that if we wanted those bananas, they would give them to us and remain hungry. The sarcastic remark made us feel guilty and we came back empty handed.

We were done with the so-called dinner and Manoj sent Neha to call us into the hanger as people sitting next to them had left and the place was vacant.

Our entire group rushed in and we all had to squeeze ourselves into the tiniest forms to adjust in the space meant for 2 or 3 people only. Somehow we managed and then I got lucky to share a little corner of a lady's shawl. I thanked God for that blessed piece of warm cloth.

Parth and I clung to each other like one soul in two bodies. We were lying on the naked floor and the mass of human forms in the hanger was shivering so much that we could hear not only ourselves but also others trying to control their chattering teeth. The cold shot into our bodies from the floor turning our flesh blue. Every single minute intensified the uncontrollable shivers and sheer pain.

I have seen many Hindi and English movies featuring trekkers on Himalayas. I was never able to imagine the degree of cold they suffered. Movies, even if based on true stories, can never make us really feel the agony of the sufferer. No one can gauge the searing chill of the bare land that we felt in the hanger that night.

Every minute seemed like a *yuga.

After an hour, the lady next to me got up and asked me if I could accompany her to the washroom. I went with her, as I didn't have the courage to say no to the benevolent soul who had been sharing her shawl with me.

The coldest breeze was blowing outside and we struggled to keep going. Still, we walked ahead somehow.

The scene outside was heart breaking.

The helipad was overflowing with thousands of shivering people.

We proceeded to the washrooms but were aghast to see people lying outside the toilet doors in a place reeking with filthy and foul smells.

Nobody seemed to be bothered by the thought that they could fall sick in that unhygienic area. But the covered washroom corridor was more than enough for these people to lie down and save themselves from the unbearable cold outside.

We saw a girl of around seven or eight years, who was vomiting outside the toilet, being heckled and yelled at by those around. They were screaming at her mother to take her somewhere else as it was already awful there and the smell of vomit was adding to it.

The girl's mother retaliated, "My daughter is not well. For God's sake show some compassion at least."

We couldn't relieve ourselves in that pathetic place.

So we looked around but couldn't find even the tiniest space to relieve ourselves anywhere as people had occupied every little corner available.

So, we decided to climb up a nearby hilly area.

The moment we started uphill, an army man appeared and very forcefully pushed us back saying that the path led to a forest that was frequently visited by wild animals.

He led us to a dirty corner and we relieved ourselves there. On the way back, we both kept talking about what kind of wild animals infested that area and what could have happened to us if that soldier hadn't warned us. I couldn't get the picture of being in the jaws of an animal out of my mind.

It was so cold outside that we were unable to move our frozen feet fast enough. But we pushed towards the hanger with all the strength we could muster.

The open area was like a scene from a horror movie. People lying on that spine chillingly bare land, all shivering and trembling. Little babies clung to their mothers desperately.

A man accidentally stepped on the stomach of a sleeping person in that darkness. The other man pushed and abused him. In another corner, some people were quarrelling over a piece of cloth. They had pulled a curtain from one of the office rooms and were fighting over it.

Those people were suffering much more than us as it was still dark outside and no one was able to see anything.

We stepped ahead very cautiously not wanting to harm or hurt anybody. Somehow we returned to our respective places inside.

That brutal night was so long I wondered if it would ever be over. We passed it just by clinging to one another for whatever warmth we could get.

The thought of wild animals and the quarrelling outside made us keep still and not get involved in any new ventures. We dropped every thought to doing anything and resigned ourselves to fate.

The night passed somehow.

CHAPTER 13

12th September 2014

At dawn, the next level in the survival game commenced.

We brushed our teeth with the little toothpaste I had and gulped the froth again. Our throats and stomachs were like a famine-struck land.

The minty taste of that small Colgate toothpaste was absolutely divine. So many times I felt like swallowing whatever was left in the tube because its fragrance and freshness moistened my system. But I controlled myself, as we had to save it for future.

Suddenly, the very pleasant noise of the chopper attracted my attention. We trooped out to the helipad to see who was boarding that day. But as soon as we stepped out we were dumbstruck. The sight was such an unbelievable one!

Instead of the Police, the whole area had been taken over by a massive number of the Indian army *jawans and officers. The senior guys were closely inspecting each part of the area and directing their subordinates on how to regulate the widespread crowd.

The breeze too felt quite pleasant.

On inquiring what was going on, we learnt authorities had realised that such a massive gathering of flood victims could in no way be handled by the local police and administration despite their sincere efforts. So the responsibility had been handed over to the Indian army.

It amazed me because when I went to the loo last night with the lady, there was no sign of this large contingent. So when did so many soldiers and officers arrive and take over the proceedings so silently and efficiently?

Everyone was surprised.

Vague theories flew about––they must have arrived in the early hours of the morning. But how come nobody heard even the faintest noise of the choppers or of their coming and that too with so many guns, riffles, ration and other supplies? How did they sneak in so stealthily?

Undoubtedly, this is the hallmark of the Indian army. They go about the task at hand so silently and with such precision. Even with thousands of people around, no one saw or heard anything of their movements in the night.

The sight of army men managing the crowd so well aroused hope in our deadened souls. Within minutes of laying eyes on them, everybody was assured that the right time had finally begun.

Fear subsided all around as people witnessed order and discipline being enforced. We all waited for something good to come out of this development.

While the army went about its task, I wandered off behind the hanger and saw around 4-5 boys climbing uphill to a little height. It made me very curious about where they were going and why. Had they found some shortcut to reach ... somewhere?

I started following them. Though the pain in my ankle bogged me down, curiosity kept me going. The boys were moving fast, as if they had found some hidden treasure like Alibaba.

But there was no such treasure. Instead, I saw them approaching a big black tank of water. The boys hurriedly went to it. One of them quickly removed the cover, peering inside the tank with anticipation, hoping to see water inside. But to their extreme dismay, it was empty to the very bottom.

They didn't give up easily though and slanted the tank to one side and opened its tap. They got 2-3 fistfuls of water. The boys, on realising that I had followed them, treated me like an equal participant in their risky adventure. They shared some of that precious water with me.

It was pale, yellowish and smelly. It must have been lying at the bottom of the abandoned tank for quite a long time. Nobody bothered about the dirt though and swallowed it immediately. We didn't bother that we could fall sick drinking that stale and stinking water. At that time, it was just water and it seemed sacred to us. Though it couldn't quench our thirst, it certainly wet our dried throats.

On getting rejuvenated, I came back to the hanger and heard Parth looking for me, "Mummy, come here fast!

The Army staff is issuing tokens to the crowd and *jijaji* has told us to get in the queue for tokens as soon as possible."

We rushed towards the helipad but it had been totally sealed, prohibiting entry for anyone. A large contingent of soldiers was guarding every single inch of that area.

The whole crowd outside the helipad was made to stand in a queue so long that the beginning point could be seen but no one had a clue where it ended.

Many officers were sitting at the entrance of the helipad and were issuing tokens to that crowd as per their turns.

First the officer would enquire, "How many members are with you?" Then he would issue one token to that family, with the number of members written on it.

The tokens were issued to the families and not to individuals, so that they could control the situation better. Their system of working was quite impressive.

The people who had been sitting on the helipad since last night waiting for their turns had been divided into groups of ten. Six such groups were made to sit in queues manned by the *jawans.

Whenever a chopper landed, only people in the first row were allowed to board. The next row would then take their place in the front. No one was allowed to go to the helipad as it disturbed smooth take off.

The officers were very strict but polite too. They were comforting the groups and asking them not to panic and maintain order so that work could be done as fast as possible. Some officers asked young men to volunteer at the entrance gate.

Parth, Anshu and Sanjay, with many others, went forward to lend a helping hand as volunteers. They started managing the chaotic crowd. All volunteers requested people to stand in the queue peacefully if they wanted the officer to issue them tokens.

But some bad elements in the crowd bullied the weaker ones and snatched their place. They pushed people around and if someone opposed, they would threaten or punch them. They were unnecessarily disrupting the process.

Parth and Anshu, while managing the crowd, succeeded in making Anju stand at the beginning of the queue.

Manoj, Neha and Radhu were almost in the middle and I was taking care of Aaru who was insisting he wanted to take a close look at the choppers. He kept crying and demanding that he be allowed to stand with Parth at the entrance.

For sometime it was okay with me but when he started running around after Parth, I went to Neha and said, "I'm losing patience with your naughty Aaru. I can't bear him anymore and I might end up yelling at him. You handle him and I'll sit in your place."

When we tried to swap places, people nearby objected vehemently. They didn't allow me to get into the line. In fact, everybody had become oversensitive and aggressive and was not ready to disturb the line at any cost because the chances of catching the chopper seemed so near.

So Aaru, the naughty boy, was again forced on me, this time he was more mischievous than before. He made me run after him continuously with my injured and aching leg. Many times I felt like slapping him but every time he would just grin and melt my heart.

This way, the two of us remained out of the queue.

Sanjay was volunteering at the queue near the helipad entrance. Whenever he got a chance, he would approach the same officer who had promised to help us get clearance the previous day.

He would request him to issue a token to our group. The officer was not easily swayed. On the contrary, he rebuked Sanjay a few times. At one point he said harshly, "Only if you really want to volunteer, then stand here. Otherwise, don't mess with the system. You'll be given token when your turn comes."

Though the officer did want to help, thousands of staring eyes didn't permit him to do anything under the table.

Sanjay had to volunteer normally again but he would keep repeating his request whenever he sighted the officer.

That day was a comforting one in many ways. With the arrival of the army and the introduction of the token system the chaos was somewhat reduced. Then, after so many days of fasting, everyone received two slices of bread per family.

We also got our share of two slices, one of which I gave to Aaru who immediately jumped to grab it and devoured it in seconds. Even after that, he kept staring at the other slice greedily.

The sight filled my eyes with tears. We raise our kids so affectionately and try our best to shower on them all the luxuries within our reach. The pampered little boy was reduced to hungering after a plain slice of bread, which perhaps he never even touches back home.

But I shared the second slice with other members. I saw people jumping over others to grab more than their share of slices from the person distributing them.

After some time, the supply of bread became more frequent. We also managed to get many slices and chewed on them savouring each bite. But we didn't stop and tried to take more to stock for the future.

We had stuffed our dirty pockets with many slices but we were finding it difficult to stop even after that. It was tough to believe we had enough.

Without considering that our pockets were caked with mud, we advised all members of the group to do the same. When the supply stemmed, we ate those sand covered slices with relish.

I didn't find it easy to chew the plain piece as it didn't easily pass through my parched throat and got stuck there. I needed some water to push it down to my stomach. But I knew water was not going to be available. So I slowly swallowed each bite somehow.

It was not just me, everyone seemed to be going through the same struggle. I saw a child drop a slice on the ground and then immediately pick it up and put the soiled bread in his mouth without any complaints.

Young, old, child, adult—all had become accustomed to eating whatever was available, paying no mind to it being filthy and dirty.

At that time 'food' was most important, not the 'quality'.

As soon as we finished our breakfast, we heard an amazing announcement. "Please come and a make a queue behind the hanger. We are distributing biscuits and namkeen packets."

It was turning out to be quite a 'food day'. But there was always a condition attached to getting even a mouthful. It was, as usual, maintaining order and discipline.

The news which should have brought some joy and relaxation for the hungry crowd, proved out to be a complete nuisance.

Last evening's *poori* incident had made the crowd wary. Nobody was ready to sit quietly anymore or follow orders. The perfectly organised mass started rushing madly in the direction of the announcement.

I handed over Aaru to Neha and went to see whether something of that kind was really being distributed or they were again rumours like last night. I took Anju with me after assurances from people that they would let her take her place when she returned.

In the lawn where biscuits and mixture packets were really being distributed, there was also a very long queue. The food-deprived crowd had gotten very impatient and the aroma of food fuelled chaos. People were pushing about to get packets first.

The army was trying to control the uncontrollable rush. The queue broke hundreds of times and they made the mob form of a line again and again.

Some people, even after getting the packets, were not ready to leave and hankered for more. That slowed down the line considerably. Only a handful were grabbing packets again and again and the rest were looking wretched and helpless.

We also looked forward to getting some for us but because of the pushing and shoving, we were unable to reach the starting point and remained at the same position.

From the queue, I noticed an old man trying to move as fast as he could to join the line. But only after a few steps he started panting heavily. His wife made him sit on a pavement and asked him not to exert himself any more. She went to fetch the eatables alone.

While I was watching the couple, Anju nudged me and told me that it was our turn, so we took our packets and started on our way back. We had got two packets each. I asked Anju to call Neha and Radhu too so that they could also get their share. Anju went to call them and I came again to stand at the end of the queue, reserving a place for them.

My eyes automatically strayed to that old man and I noticed that he was constantly staring at food in other people's hands. Then he got up and tried to find a place in the line. But due to his age and frailty, he couldn't tolerate the pushing from the strong crowd. In spite of getting closer to the men who were distributing the packets, he got pushed out of the queue.

I became really concerned for him.

Anju brought Neha and Radhu who took their places in the queue. I went to sit on the same pavement beside him. I don't know what tempted me to talk to that man and I asked him, "Uncle, where are you from?"

"From Delhi, *beta*," he replied.

He also put the same question to which I said, "I'm also from Delhi."

We struck up a conversation.

He told me that he and his wife had come to Kashmir a fortnight ago for the Amarnath *Yatra*[118] for the first time. But he suffered an asthma attack and had to be hospitalised for 10 days. The doctors forbade him from going to the *yatra*[119]. They were planning to go back to Delhi when suddenly the flood hit and they got stranded. He rued that since stepping into Kashmir they had been hurtling from one problem to the next and suffering the worst kind of fate.

In the meanwhile, his wife came back empty handed, saying that it was impossible for her to reach the distribution point.

Their story really touched me and I said, "Uncle, you take these two packets. I'll again stand in the queue."

Though I had offered magnanimously, while handing over the packets I felt as if I was letting go of something very precious. My hungry kids were also waiting, after all. How could I give their share to this couple? But I had been moved by their plight and I had promised. Without any further thoughts, I simply gave them the packets.

In return, they gave me a thousand blessings and I stood up to get back in the queue. When I narrated the whole story to Anju and Neha, they didn't object at all but consoled me, "Don't worry mausiji, we have collected enough packets. You go and pass these packets to Manoj, Parth, Anshu and Sanjay."

---

[118] *pilgrimage*
[119] *pilgrimage*

I left but could only find Manoj. I came back and sent Radhu to find the other three.

We found it impossible to believe that better time was slowly approaching. The previous day, we had tasted the flavour of wheat and now our tongues were enjoying the deliciousness of the salt.

God bless Mr. Narendra Modi who had made arrangements to supply that Gujarati mixture to the hungry mob. All started shouting, "Narendra Modi *zindabad*."[120]

It was a spontaneous outpouring from everybody's hearts, so we also joined the shouting. Whatever their political beliefs, people were showering heaps of blessings on him.

Actually, anyone who made arrangements for us that day would have been the recipient of our blessings and gratitude.

After collecting the packets, we came back to our queue but it had come to a standstill. Anju was trying to pull me too into the queue with her but people were getting irritated by the additions. So they didn't let me in.

The whole scenario had changed. Nobody was letting people who had left to collect packets to re-join the queue again. Though people reasoned that they had been in the line only a while back, the crowd was adamant and dismissed all valid reasons.

---

[120] *long live*

This happened with Neha and Radhu too, when they returned to their places after collecting their packets. They were not allowed to get in and were told to go to the end of the queue again.

Everything got messed up. Quarrels began. Manoj started fighting with people saying that Neha and Radhu had been sitting there already and they had only got up to get food. He defended them, "Why should they go at the back again, when I have been sitting here for them? They should get their respective places back with no arguments."

But nobody honoured his logic. In fact, they argued that they hadn't gone to collect their packets though they were starving too. If others left the queue, then they had to face the consequences.

A lot of pushing and shoving ensued.

The volunteers tried to settle the quarrel as the queue was under their supervision. Most of the army staff was busy at the helipad so this place was left entirely in the hands of the volunteers. Even after their best efforts, they were not able to control the crowd.

At this point Sanjay rushed to call us, "There is no need to sit in the queue. I have taken the tokens. Let's be fast. we have to sit in the queues at the helipad now."

We asked him, "How did you manage to get it?"

He replied, "I was constantly asking the senior officer a token for nine members. After much persuasion, finally I got one token but for three people only."

He added, "I continued asking for one more token for six members but the officer had a token for five people in his hand and pitying me, he passed that to me stealthily."

Sanjay then sent Parth to request the same officer, "Sir, eight members have got tokens and only I'm left. Please issue me one token for myself."

But the officer recognised Parth was with Sanjay. He lost his cool this time and shouted, "Go away boy! I have already done so much for you people. If you want those tokens then keep them, else I'll take them too." Parth came back defeated.

Sanjay asked all of us to hurry. "What about you, how will you come?" we asked. He said, "I'll manage. At least you all go." And he forced us to leave without him.

With the tokens, we reached the helipad. There was a huge rush but it was being well managed. Entry to those six queues was strictly according to token numbers. The staff was checking very carefully the number of members written on each token. The whole area was strictly under their vigilance. They were regulating the crowd very well.

After such a long battle, we were sure that no matter what the circumstances, we would at least be able to catch a chopper that day.

Since we had two tokens, three members of the first token (Radhu, Neha and Aaru) were made to sit in the first queue and the rest (Manoj, Anshu, Anju, Parth and I) in the last queue. We sat there silently. Though we were in different queues, none of us made any fuss about wanting to be together. It was a great relief to find ourselves on that most sought after patch of land.

It felt like after a long pilgrimage we had finally reached the doors of our temple and we were waiting for the holy priest to permit us to put our feet into the sanctum sanctorum. The only difference was that our temple was not on land; it was a flying chopper.

We had prayed every second since we were in CH2 for this moment. And when the moment was nearing, we could hardly wait. We were wondering why the chopper was taking so much time and when we would get to board it.

All of us were constantly counting the number of people who were sitting before us and estimated that after about 8-10 flights roughly, it would be our turn.

Each chopper was taking 10-12 people and around 80-90 people were sitting ahead of us and almost the same number or a little more were sitting behind us. We were in the middle of the queues. Minute after minute the wait was becoming more difficult.

Suddenly a chopper landed and four army men came out of it with crates of mineral water bottles.

Everyone immediately started shouting, "Water! Water!"

People who had been sitting silently till now started getting up to see where the water was being taken. The *jawans* sternly ordered them to keep sitting in their places, else they would throw them out of the queue.

We saw *jawans* bring the crates to us and we couldn't believe our eyes. It had been so many days that we had seen a full bottle of crystal clear water. Suddenly there were so many before our eyes!

Those bottles were distributed among people in the queues. They gave one bottle to each family and people jumped to grab them. We got two and immediately shared them among us.

After many days, we were been able to quench our thirst. It was more than life saving nectar to us and we enjoyed every single drop. Our moisture-deprived bodies finally felt rejuvenated.

Some people weren't satisfied with just one bottle and by hook or crook they acquired some extra bottles. Parth also got one extra bottle by requesting the man who was distributing them and then quickly hid it in his bag. It was not the first time we had done that, but by then, we had mastered the hoarding game. We had been reduced to thieves and burglars and had become extremely selfish living the game of survival.

Whatever we got, we aspired to get more. The trust in our fate was totally lost. In our hearts, it was difficult to accept that we would soon be reaching home soon.

The choppers were coming at regular intervals and every one of them was bringing water bottles, biscuits, blankets and milk for babies. The staff went around asking families if they had any small kid. Milk was then supplied in small glasses. They took good care not only of the crowd at the helipad but distributed the same things among people standing in long queues outside the helipad.

We felt that finally everything was in order. The army would be able to maintain discipline and that would ensure every single soul was dispatched to their respective hometowns.

But a horrifying incident made the whole crowd cagey and restless.

All of a sudden, one of the five middle-aged men sitting in the last row became unconscious due to the heat, which he was not able to bear. One of his group members requested the staff, "Sir, our friend has suffered from a heat stroke and he is in a very serious condition. Please, let us go first."

The staff was sympathetic and allowed them to come in the first row. But while they were shifting, some people objected and demanded that only the sick man should be allowed to board the chopper out of turn but not his friends.

Some people tried to go along with them pretending to be part of the group. When the army realised what was happening, they tried to stop it. This made the whole system go awry. Hot arguments flared up and the crowd became uncontrollable.

Someone told us that two groups had fought among themselves on some issue and one man had hit the other and the latter was seriously injured. The intensity of the time was too grave that nobody bothered about the reason but wished to provide some first aid to the injured. Two army jawaans hurriedly took the injured man to a cabin to treat him.

The rest of the crowd, which was siting silently, scattered in all directions. We were back to square one.

The staff arranged a chopper quickly and the wounded man along with his family was taken to the airport. Even after witnessing all this, two-three people still tried to board the same chopper. The staff pushed them back and the chopper took off.

The news was rife that the man had died on the spot but to avoid any further unrest, the matter was hushed up very fast.

The condition was that the idle brains were weaving this or that sort of stories. Hardly anyone knew there was a bit of truth in them but it was simply adding some spice in the boring routine of bootless waiting.

Few only were applauding the way army was bridling the masses.

The army had to redouble its efforts to bring the scared and wild crowd under control. This time the mob sat silently and didn't engage in any sort of arguments.

As a result, choppers landed smoothly and officers sent people line after line quickly.

A few people started taking pictures of that time. We also captured a few shots with our Digicams. Those were after all unusual and unforgettable moments of our life.

Normally, whenever we click a pic, or take a selfie, we are very conscious of our looks, dress, hairstyle and angles and we pose to look our best. That day we looked terrible. For the last six days we had been in muddy clothes, we hadn't washed our faces, and not combed our hair. Strands had become stiff like twigs and it was impossible for the bristles of the comb to reach the scalp.

But the situation was entirely different from normal time. We had reached a state of joy after undergoing a hellish week. So very happily, we posed for pics in our worn out condition.

Soon, the sun came overhead and its scorching heat became unbearable. Our bodies started itching because sand under our clothes dried. It became very difficult to pass a moment more in those clothes in which we had been living for so many days. They had become hard like a shell and the dry sand began pouring out automatically. Rashes on arms and legs made us extremely itchy.

See how strange it is…

We had suffered so much worse in the last few days. We had never acted restlessly as our entire attention was on escaping the immediate horror––the flood in CH2, passing through broken windows bruising our bodies, crossing the deadly passage over water holding the railing, getting thrown through another window risking our life every second, waiting endlessly for the boat and then struggling to get in one, fighting the leak in the boat, the struggle at the army camp to send a boat to CH2 for the men, the chill at Jayeshta Devi Temple, the enormous struggle to enter the main gate at the helipad, passing two frozen nights at the helipad without food and water and finally the struggle to get a token for the choppers.

But as soon as we received confirmation that we were out of danger, we not only relaxed but began fussing about clothes, food and other conveniences.

This is human nature. We are never satisfied with our present condition and always aspire for more.

We were now counting the number of passengers ahead of us again and again and thankfully with every hour their numbers were reducing. Finally, we moved from being in the middle rows to the first two lines.

Then arrived the long-awaited moment––our turn to get into the chopper. At first, it was Radhu's turn as she was in the first row. Neha and Aaru couldn't go with her because there was only one seat vacant. And after that shooting incident, everyone was too scared to demand they wanted to go only with their family. No one dared utter a single word to disrupt the smooth functioning of the system.

When her turn came, we willingly sent her under the guidance of other people in the chopper. Our motto at that time was to send whomsoever we could. At least he or she would be able to reach a safer place.

After Radhu's departure, more choppers started landing one by one at very short intervals. The enormous sea of people, though at a very slow speed, started receding. The lines were finally moving fast.

We relaxed and started chit-chatting with other people sitting nearby who also seemed equally relieved. All were of the opinion that if the mob had let the army do its work peacefully earlier, then the whole situation wouldn't have become so bad. But we unnecessarily created so many issues, disrupting speedy evacuation.

Our only worry was to see Sanjay with us. Again and again we turned our heads to see whether he had gotten entry to the helipad or not. We wanted to request the officers to let him come but nobody dared to. The staff was very busy and barely had time to listen to individual requests. Actually, they were focussed on transporting the maximum number of people that day and couldn't afford any disturbance. So, we honoured their decision.

Suddenly, we saw Sanjay entering, holding an old man's hand. He was making his way to us.

When he came fully into view, we were astonished. The old man was the same gentleman who had come for Amarnath *Yatra*[121] and to whom I had given my share of biscuit packets.

Sanjay was escorting the old couple with utmost care. Our eyes met and he waved and he assured us that there was nothing to worry about and he would be joining us at Jammu Military Airbase.

On seeing that old man, I thanked God that he had rewarded me for my small act of kindness by sending Sanjay to them.

Our turn finally came. All of us except Sanjay were to take that flight. And the moment arrived just like that––the chopper landed and the officers asked us to move forward. My whole body was shivering due to excitement. We at once rose and started running wildly as we were not sure of our luck and still feared we could be dragged back to stay in that hell. The harsh sound of the engine was music to our ears. We had waited so long in anticipation of this moment.

We moved ahead very cautiously, keeping our heads and bodies slightly bent so that we didn't get hurt by its enormous wings that were hovering overhead. In fact, the army men were very alert when people were boarding. They helped them in climbing successfully without any mishap.

Finally all of us were in the chopper––it was 12th September 2014, 12:40 p.m.

_____

[121] *pilgrimage*

We clung to each other and waved to Sanjay and other people who were left behind on the helipad waiting for their turn. We were ecstatic and made signs of victory. We were certain that Sanjay would be joining us in no time.

From the chopper, we viewed the helipad for the last time. Lakhs of refugees were sitting there hoping to soon be in our position. The helipad, which had been a place of complete disorder and chaos only a few hours back, had now turned into a disciplined zone.

As we moved away from the helipad and came over the valley, my body froze. The aerial view of the drowned area belied that it was the same Kashmir about whose beauty poets and writers have written songs, poems and books, and musicians have sung thousands of songs in its praise.

A valley upon which nature has bestowed a marvellous bounty of dense forests; picturesque landscapes with snow-capped mountain peaks; aromatic tea-gardens and orchards of juicy apples, peaches, plums and walnuts; glorious Shalimar and Nishat gardens; and wild fauna like deer, bear, rabbits, owls––a place christened Heaven on Earth.

A state whose people are famous for their hospitality and politeness towards their guests, which we had enjoyed many times during our trips; whose delicate tone of speech with a mix of Urdu and Kashmiri language made everyone fall in love with them; where every season, tourists from all walks of life and from every part of the world flocked to enjoy the soul-searing beauty and enrich themselves with its rich heritage.

None of this was anywhere to be seen.

Houses, buildings, houseboats, temples, vehicles, trees and people––all were partially submerged in water. We saw a few people trying to wade through the flood with the help of a rope. Many people were siting on the terrace of their houses, waving their *duppattas*[122] or *sarees*[123] or any other piece of cloth to signal for help. Many locals were being rescued by both army and civilian boats.

Not even a single square feet of that vast land looked dry. Only water was visible, which had engulfed the heritage-rich and beautiful valley completely, forcing the sweet and innocent inhabitants to face serious repercussions and leave their dear motherland.

It looked as if Indra, the God of rain and thunder, had taken an oath to prove his might. We have heard that Indra sustains life, but when he rages, he impairs it.

We see these two roles played by the Lord of water in our lives––the life giving one and the life taking one. Without his grace, no life is possible on the earth but in Kashmir we witnessed him in all his fury.

In anger, he flooded the entire valley in the blink of an eye. He shook the foundations of things that man thought could never be shaken––monuments, gardens, skyscrapers, railways, dams, villages, hospitals, hotels, roads. Everything

[122] *veil*
[123] *saris*

became vulnerable, lost its firm grip and was sucked into the flood's deep belly. Nothing but water was visible for as far as one could see.

Lord Indra's power was in full display. One should never underestimate His might as He is the highest authority on earth and all should bow down to his sovereignty.

Within 15 minutes of taking off from the helipad we had reached the JK Army Airport. As we landed, the terror, the signs of fear and depression dissipated.

Quite a few soldiers helped us disembark safely. When our chopper became empty, another batch of soldiers brought cartons of water bottles, food, baby food packets, blankets and basic medicines which they loaded in the same chopper for the refugees who were still on the helipad. They were operating with clockwork precision and performing their duties as fast as they could.

It looked as if they were in more haste to help the refugees than the refugees themselves.

We finally entered the airport and our jaws dropped.

We stood staring at a huge multitude of hungry and tired people waiting desperately to be sent home.

CHAPTER 14

Around 1 p.m.

The army staff welcomed us warmly and registered our names again to ensure the list of rescued victims was updated constantly.

Immediately after that, we were given fresh water bottles, namkeen and bananas to eat. Every single person coming in was received with great sympathy.

We again drank a lot of water and ate more than one packet of mixture each. After that, we were given some *poori and *aloo sabzi[124]. When we opened the packets, we realized that the curry was stale. Even so, we couldn't resist the temptation of eating *poori and sabzi, and devoured it hungrily. We kept binging on them till our stomachs started aching due to overeating.

All the time, we had been worrying about Sanjay. We kept counting how many choppers had landed since we came and finally after four rounds, Sanjay also arrived with the same old couple.

---

[124] *potato curry*

We rushed to receive him and enveloped him in a group embrace.

Soon we asked him, "How did you meet this couple?"

He told us that when he was trying to convince the officer to allot a token for a single person, he came across that old couple. During a conversation they realized that not only were all from Delhi, surprisingly they were from the same colony—the spice market of Chandni Chowk in Old Delhi!

Sanjay then told them that eight members of his family had gone and he was left alone. The couple offered, "'*Beta*, you come with us. We'll ask for a token for three. If anyone questions, we will say you are our son."

They were given a token for three members without much questioning. We all thanked uncle and aunty profusely for their help.

They were very astonished to find that Sanjay belonged to my family. We all became the Delhite group. Once they received water and eatables, we sat together in the garden and enjoyed the sunny day.

Many reporters from various channels came to interview us. Manoj and I talked to them and told them the tale of our miseries. We didn't hide anything. Whatever legal or illegal we had witnessed in those chaotic days—the inability of the local police proved to be effective because of limited staff, the local peoples' solidarity and to some extent the resulting anarchy, the heroism of our brave and beloved army and the aid provided by our honourable Prime Minister Mr. Modi to the hunger-stricken mob.

They clicked many pictures and promised that the recording would be telecast the same night and our family members would be able to see us since they would be following the news closely in Delhi.

They interviewed many other groups also and almost all had the same views. Some of them were still so tense that they said, "Sir, the local Kashmiri people do not have faith in the Indian army despite all its efforts to protect them. Hence the situation became even more tough to control."

The reporters jotted down every single word from different groups giving them enough time to speak their minds. Some reporters interviewed a few Kashmiris who had also been rescued with us. But it was astonishing that only a few spoke well of our *jawans* and others didn't utter a single word in appreciation of the army that had rescued them. They kept mum when the media asked them their views in this regard. The others, though, not only praised the *jawans* but also showered heaps of blessings on them.

They face enormous hardships to ensure the safety and security of all the citizens of India. Our *jawans* are angels in the guise of men.

Whenever a crisis arises
They sacrifice their lives!

Though we were at the final stage of our survival game, we were still not sure when we would go home. We kept our fingers crossed so that nothing ominous would befall us. And we prayed asking God to send our aircraft soon so that we could rejoin our families.

On reaching the airport, Sanjay went to charge his mobile so that he could tell people back home that we had reached the airport safely. He, in all aspects, proved to be a hero for us. He did all he could to rescue our group. He was a genuine person who hardly cared for himself and shouldered his responsibilities with absolute commitment and conviction. He could visualize forthcoming problems and would figure out some solution to the comfort of our entire group.

When he reached the charging point, there was a huge rush there. Everybody was in a great haste to inform their families about their safety.

But even after charging the battery for around 20-30%, some people were refusing to let others charge their phones. Yet again harsh words were exchanged.

To avoid more chaos, *jawans* took many people to their offices to provide them with charging sets. These sets were getting power supply through generators, which had been brought from other states.

Sanjay also got his mobile charged a little and called his father to share the good news that we all had reached the JK Army Airport and we might land at Delhi Army Airport in a few hours.

When his father heard his voice, he broke down on the phone and kept weeping. He informed Sanjay that he had done everything in his power to get us out safely. He had offered a crore of rupees or more to anyone who could bring us back safely. He went to as many people in power as he could find to ask them if they could do anything to get us out of Kashmir.

But they all said the same thing––they were helpless since the entire state was in the grip of a monumental crisis.

Even after that, he sent Sanjay's younger brother Ashok to JK Airport to try and see if anybody could do something to bring us back.

He had given Ashok instructions not to worry about money and simply focus on our safe return. But when Ashok landed at the airport, he realized how bad the situation was. The entire valley had drowned leaving only the airport safe.

Even so, he tried to grease the palms of the concerned authorities but on being convinced that nothing could be done, he returned to Delhi dejected. Since then, all our family members had been running from pillar to post to discover our whereabouts.

And after a number of days of no news, came the moment when Sanjay informed them of our wellbeing. After Sanjay, my turn came and I called Kashish. He very excitedly screamed, "Mumma! Where are you? Are you OK?"

I told him, "Yes baby, we all are OK. Now we are at Jammu Military Airbase. Today, by evening perhaps, we will catch our flight to Delhi."

"Okay Mumma. I'm coming to Delhi Airport and I am bringing a lot of food and cold drinks for all of you," he replied.

I had heard my son's happy voice after many days.

I was craving to pour my heart out to him. I was sure that he would be equally eager to see Parth and me after seven days of dashed hopes. I just wanted us to become a united family again.

Soon we heard that since the maximum numbers of passengers were to fly to Delhi, the authorities were trying to arrange for a big aircraft, which was not available at the present hour. The officers informed us that more passengers for Delhi were expected from the helipad. Only after all people bound for the capital reached the airport, would the aircraft take off.

Then began a round of hoping that more and more Delhi passengers would arrive so that we could leave soon. We went around asking people whether they were from Delhi and whenever they said yes, we would feel happy.

While waiting, we met Deepak, an army man, who told us that he was going to his village near Rohtak. I was surprised to see an army man going back to his village at a time when the nation needed him. But I didn't voice my concern.

While everybody else was very enthusiastic about going back, Deepak seemed to be sad and sat very still. He didn't show any signs of happiness or desire to head home.

He was sitting silently near our group. Again and again someone or the other was going to the offices to ask whether the aircraft had come, but he never showed any such eagerness. His behaviour surprised us all.

To the repeated enquires from people, the authorities always said that the flight to Delhi would depart after a bigger plane had been arranged, which would probably take a few hours. We had no option left but to suffer the endless hours of waiting.

Deepak lay down on the grass to wait.

Earlier, trapped in CH2, we didn't have any idea what we were waiting for. But now the goal was clear to us––our final flight that would take us home. Being aware of this next step somehow made it tougher to stay still and wait. So close to our destination, our restlessness to leave was of another kind.

But no signal from the authorities was forthcoming.

One by one, more evacuees kept landing and they were also adjusted at the airport like us. The place was brimming over with thousands of people. Many of them had already become known to us as we had all been struggling for life together and had made progress from one stage to the next at the same time.

Mannat and Mandira with their parents got down from the chopper. They were very happy to see us and said, "Finally, we made it safely."

I asked their mother, "When did you reach the helipad? We looked for you."

She replied, "We entered the main gate the afternoon after you did and that too after a lot of pleading with the officers. We spent the whole day and night on the open helipad. Mandira has caught fever due to the extreme chill."

We were still sharing our stories when the announcement for the Chandigarh flight was heard. On hearing it Mannat asked her mother to hurry up as they had to board the plane to Chandigarh.

We quickly bade them goodbye.

We had mixed feelings––on the one hand we were happy that finally they were escaping hell; on the other, we were upset because there were yet no announcements for the Delhi flight.

One after the other, a large number of people were being sent away to their respective destinations be it Jammu, Chandigarh, Lucknow or Gujarat. Whenever the announcements were made, we longed to hear, "Passengers for Delhi". But how could we be so lucky? Whenever people boarded their planes, their faces lit up with happiness. We were dying to experience that bliss.

Having nothing to do, we started roaming aimlessly in the vicinity to kill time. The army airport had many big fighter aircrafts parked. We were astonished to see the majesty of those aircrafts. They were gigantic and even their sight frightened us. We just stood there appreciating the marvellous machines.

If it had been a pleasant time, we might have felt honoured to see the army airport and the fighter aircrafts. It is a protected area where no civilian can come without permission. But the situation was exactly the opposite that day. The *jawans* were fewer in number compared to the civilians. The whole airport, its offices, its gardens, its canteen and even the runway was occupied by ordinary people.

The icing on the cake was that officers and *jawans* were all the time ready to serve us. They were making us feel that we were no less than valuable guests to them.

But we were focused only on one thing and it was getting on our nerves. The delay in the arrival of our aircraft rattled us more and more with every passing hour. We did not want to stay there anymore, but had to. We wanted to fly high in the sky but felt that our wings had been snipped.

For sometime we all sat in the garden but the sun came overhead and we got very irritable. I got up to find some shady area.

Guess what I found?

In a corner I saw a tap with running water!

Was it really a tap I was seeing? I couldn't believe my eyes! Undoubtedly it was real and not a hallucination.

I had seen a tap after so many dry days, so I ran to it to feel clean, running water through my fingers. As soon as I touched those drops, I felt electrified. I felt it again and again in my hands. Oh, God! What a wonderful feeling that was!

Though my body did not need any more water as I had already had a lot, how could I let the charm of drinking straight from the tap slip by? I cupped my hands together and let the sacred *amrit*[125] revive my soul.

I don't remember how much water I let slip down my throat, but I didn't stop till my belly started aching. From the corner of my eye, I saw a small piece of soap lying in a muddy corner. Someone might have thrown it away finding it too small to be used anymore. I quickly picked it up and immediately applied it on my hands and face. I inhaled the fragrance deeply, as it was such a sublime experience after having lived through so many stenches.

When I splashed water on my face, the layers of mud started coming off my skin. So did the layers of the toothpaste foam, which were deposited one over the other. All those days, we had brushed with paste on our fingers and gulped the foam, the residual froth drying on the sides of our lips and faces. Half of that precious toothpaste was still safe in my pocket. I had always taken good care of it.

---

[125] *nectar*

I washed my face again and again and continued the process till I got tired.

I used up that little soap cleaning myself. I didn't even think of sharing it with anybody else. Only when I was done with drinking from the tap and cleaning myself did I think of calling others. One by one, I showed them the way to this little piece of heaven. Parth and Anshu started searching for soap in the dirt, but couldn't find any.

They were not as lucky as I was!

They saw a few people picking up wet clay and scrubbing it on their hands and faces. After rubbing, they washed it off and what emerged was clean shining skin underneath. The idea was just amazing and all in our group started imitating them. See the irony! After being in muddy hell for so many days, they resorted to applying clay to remove the mud caked on the skin!

After many days our faces and hands began to look familiar and resemble our original selves. We didn't have a mirror so we teased each other, "Oh, my God! You are looking so 'Clean and Clear'."

It was a pleasant way to pass time. After washing our faces, we put our heads under running water. The thick layers of dirt in our hair separated from the scalp and melted. Mud came out like *henna*[126] comes out of hair while washing.

---

[126] *a reddish-brown dye made from the powdered leaves of a tropical shrub, used to colour hair and decorate body*

Having indulged in this luxury, more desires sprung up in our hearts. Wish we had shampoo, scrubbers, towels, we bemoaned! I just wanted to stand under a shower and was ready to pay a very good amount to anyone who could arrange that for me.

We all got carried away and passed quite a few luscious hours relishing every drop from the tap. When we were fresh enough and content, we sat in the shade.

Around 3 p.m.

Though our bags were stuffed with eatables––bananas, mixtures and *namakpare*, Aaru saw somebody eating Maggi. He ran to his mother and started asking for some. On inquiring, we found that we could get readymade Maggi from the army canteen.

All immediately galloped to canteen. But as usual we ran into a very long queue where people were offering ridiculous amounts to the cook for half a plate of Maggi or even less than that. But the cook refused all payment saying that he had run out of stock. After standing and quarrelling for an hour with others, we were finally lucky to get one plate of Maggi. All shared one spoon each and left the rest for Aaru.

By 5 p.m.

We saw some people eating *dal*-rice. The aroma was simply irresistible. Again the mad race began. All rushed towards to the *dal*-rice queue. It was again a never-ending one. Parth and Anshu somehow managed to get in the middle of the queue and made their way to the cash counter. They tried to bribe the cashier and the cook as well, with a note of thousand rupees so that he would give us 2-3 plates. Again they refused to take the money and snubbed the boys, asking them to be in the queue and wait for their turn.

The army personnel indeed proved to be very honest.

After waiting for a long time, we got one plate and we enjoyed every grain. But we kept craving for more.

Radhu was not feeling well, so she lay down for sometime. We were also lying or sitting listless as there was nothing to do except watch people of other states board their planes and hope our turn would come soon.

Aaru was getting restless and cried, *"Mumma ghar kab jayenge? Batao naa please."*[127]

As usual, Aaru again targeted Parth to make his life miserable. He had a newer demand and he wanted to sleep in Parth's lap.

This time, Parth allowed the hassled kid to lie in his lap but with a strict warning, "Now be absolutely quiet, else we will leave you alone here."

Aaru immediately grabbed the opportunity and drifted into a serene slumber, as if he had been lulled by a lullaby.

---

[127] *When will we go home Mom?*

We were also getting restless like Aaru as all wanted to go home as soon as possible.

By 8 p.m.

The choppers had stopped bringing more refugees as the limit for the day had been reached. They were allowed to bring only as many people as could be dispatched to their respective destinations the same day.

The passengers weren't allowed to stay in the army airport overnight due to safety reasons.

Hours crept by and the Delhi lot was trying its best to be patient. Some aggressive people got up to enquire from the staff about the aircraft. Again they got the same assurance that it was about to reach. Once again we sat subdued. We didn't want to disrupt the on going process and the same continued till 10 p.m.

All the flights had taken off, except the one to Delhi.

The temperature began falling as darkness fell. We started turning cold not only due to the weather but also fear. The grass had become wet and the breeze started blowing hard. We were sitting on the wet grass near the runway, shivering.

The airport was vacant. Only four big rows of Delhi passengers waited there, baffled and confused.

CHAPTER 15

13th September 2014

12 a.m.

It was midnight and the bridge of our patience collapsed. A few members got up to fight with the staff on duty. They reassured us all over again that the needful was being done on their part. But the limits of our tolerance had been breached.

We discussed amongst ourselves and rose to shout for our rights. Why was the Delhi flight not being given any importance? All screamed in unison and a few even started fighting with the men on duty.

One praiseworthy trait of the army men was that even when they were face-to-face with such a furious crowd, not one of them got angry or impatient and dealt with the agitated crowd with great expertise.

They had been around us round the clock. They were very polite and taking good care of everyone.

The army was also operating a medical camp for evacuees for preliminary treatment. They were giving medicines to the sick and needy. Parth took me to the camp and asked me to rest for a while after which I got a bit relieved.

When we came back, we saw Deepak talking to a senior officer and showing him his badge. He was requesting something and the officer was continuously saying no to him. We didn't know what the matter was.

He came back and sat beside me. I offered him something to eat as he had not eaten anything since we had come here. That broke the ice and we started to talk.

I asked him about his family. He told me that his elder brother and he were both in the army. They were in the Badami Bagh cantonment area when the flood hit. He was rescued after two days but his brother was still missing.

His father had also been in the army and during the Kargil war he had been shot. After losing her husband, his mother had to face many problems in raising her sons. Yet, she wanted them to join the Indian army so that they could continue the family tradition of dedicating their lives to the nation.

In fact, several generations of his family had been in army and navy including his grandfather and his great grandfather, who, he said, was with Gandhiji during the Dandi March at the time of the freedom movement.

His cousins and even his sisters' husbands were in the army at different posts.

I understood then why he was sad. He was worried about his brother whose whereabouts were not known. To take his mind off the subject, I started talking of how the authorities were taking too much time to arrange for the Delhi flight. He just nodded his head and said nothing.

Sanjay and Manoj repeatedly asked the officers for some quick action.

After constant requests, the staff members took our pleas seriously. They began making calls to the higher authorities and informed them that our group could no longer be disciplined. The wet grass along with the chilling breeze was making us go numb. Once again, we were facing the dreaded cold.

The anticipation and eagerness of meeting our loved ones was making us more impatient. We were in constant touch with our family members on the mobile. I got to know that Kashish, with his friend Jayesh, was waiting at the Delhi Army Airport since the time he had heard that we were at JK Airport.

It was the same with Anju and Neha's families. All had been waiting anxiously for our return since 1 p.m. It had been almost 11 hours of waiting for them too and none of them had retuned home. They had brought food for us and were constantly asking the Delhi airport authorities when the Jammu flight would come. The authorities assured them repetitively that the flight was expected any moment. But god only knows how long those hours were for them.

Some frustrated people around us started accusing the authorities, "Why are you not taking any action? Why are you holding up only Delhi passengers?" A man remarked, "Some politics is going on here!"

On hearing that statement, Deepak who had been silent till then, said, "Sir, you shouldn't say things like this. Do you know that not just the Indian army, but the air force is also doing its best to save everyone? The delay is due to the fact that the flood has devastated our facilities and camps too. Around 800 of our *jawans are stranded in the flood and are also being rescued."

He reminded us of the times the armed forces had selflessly served and protected the nation. He told us many details and stories of bravery and sacrifice.

Soon, everyone became engrossed with what he was saying. The facts Deepak shared with us encouraged the curious soul in me to ask him questions about the army and the air force.

He said that Indian armed forces take care of security outside and peace within our borders. During war, the air force supports the army by conducting aerial war and ensures that our airspace remains unbreached. Indian air force was an equal partner of the army in the Indo-Pak wars and the conflict with China.

He told us that IAF has several aircrafts. While the exact number of these aircrafts is not known, people say it is probably around 2000.

According to him, in natural calamities like flood, landslides, earthquakes etc., all three forces carry out joint search and rescue operations, follow it up by providing the rescued with shelter, food, water, medicines, blankets, tents, etc. and then go on to do long-term rehabilitation work.

In J&K also, the government had deployed all three forces in the flood-hit areas so that the rescue operation could be speeded up. Along with these forces, the National Disaster Management force was also involved in providing relief.

He was a knowledge bank and one after the other people started putting questions to him. For a while, our attention was diverted providing some relief to the airport authorities from our constant nagging.

Deepak said that he would join us in sometime and went to enquire if they had any news of his brother.

When he left, others started sharing information about the situation. Some said that they had never heard of such severe floods in Kashmir in many decades. Some others said that they had heard that all of a sudden the Jhelum and Chenab rivers were flowing above the danger mark. Hundreds of villages were affected. Many districts in Punjab and in Pakistan like Sialkot and Lahore were flooded. River Jhelum had breached its banks submerging Sonwar Bagh, Lal Chowk, Rajbagh and Wazir Bagh and neighbouring areas.

According to others, the reason for the flood could be the unchecked cutting of trees and encroachment of the riverbanks and ponds. Some people said that the disaster was a result of climate change.

Actually in some aspects, I agreed with the former. When I had visited Kashmir in 1998, there were very few houseboats on Dal Lake, but by 2014 people had grown thick aquatic plants on a major portion of the lake to turn water into land.

In the greed to grab more land, they disturbed the ecological balance of nature and the entire area had to face repercussions.

Deepak returned and joined us saying that he had requested officers to cancel his vacation and permit him to be with them to help the victims. He said he was hoping to get permission soon.

He had informed his mother and she too was pressurizing him not to come back home and to do his duty. His statement surprised all. Within a few minutes, he had become our hero.

We again surrounded him to learn more about the catastrophe. He told us that because of the flooding of the BSF headquarters and army cantonment in Badami Bagh, the search and evacuation operation was majorly hindered. There was also a shortage of boats and the districts of South Kashmir very badly affected.

I asked him where the boats in which we were rescued had come from.

He said that in these kinds of calamities, boats are airlifted from all corners of India, as they must have been this time too.

That is where the contribution of the Air Force begins Deepak said. It ferries men and equipment and airdrops food packets and medicines to trapped people. Then, once the ground forces have brought people to a safer place, it picks them in choppers and drops them at army airports from where army planes drop them to their respective state's airports.

While we had been eyewitnesses and beneficiaries of the whole process, only after talking to Deepak we could piece together the disparate experiences and see a clear picture of the recuse operation.

Deepak also told us that the Indian Navy commandos were going into the deepest and the most inaccessible parts of Kashmir to search for trapped people and bring them to safety.

He said the operation would not stop after sending the tourists home. The real work would start after water receded. Many diseases could ravage water- logged areas so a huge body of army personnel would be deployed to handle hygiene and sanitation.

He said he had witnessed one such flood in Uttarakhand only a year ago. In June 2013, clouds bursts and resulting heavy rainfalls had devastated the state. The Alaknanda river had ravaged Kedarnath, Rambara, Badrinath, Hemkund Sahib and Rudra Prayag districts.

At that time, he was in Harsil with his battalion rescuing stranded pilgrims and locals. They went to many remote areas to find affected people. Many of them were alive and many in a wretched condition, but some were dead. He and his colleagues retrieved the dead bodies and cremated them according to rituals. Some bodies were so battered that identification was impossible, but they still kept records in case someone came to claim them.

J&K was facing a similar catastrophe. Interrupting him, I asked, "Aren't you scared for your life? Being in the army, you can be asked at any time to tackle dangerous situations that put your life at risk."

He said it depends on the perspective of a person. There is no security in anyone's life. Anybody can meet their end anywhere, even sitting peacefully in the living room watching T.V.

Death is inevitable, so why to worry about it he said. Everyone will die but what matters is how he dies. When we die at war or while serving our nation, the sense of pride is above and beyond owning the world's princely treasures.

He was talking continuously and we were astonished to learn just how organized the troops were. This boy, who must be around 24-25 years old, was not creating any fuss over his lost brother. On the contrary, he said that he did not want to go back to his village in the time of distress. But his seniors were forcefully sending him back saying that his mother needed him more and they had enough staff to carry out the rescue operations.

A soldier came over to where we were sitting and said that there was a call for Deepak in the office. Deepak left with him.

In his absence, I sat stunned. Who are these people and what kind of clay are they moulded from? How can a human being be so selfless? How can a mother send her sons to join the army even after loosing her husband in war?"

I kept thinking and appreciating the way his mother had brought up her children. I had always thought that only I struggled so much to rear my kids, but only in a few hours Deepak had proved me wrong.

I don't know why, but I felt like meeting his mother and asking her how she managed all alone in this mean world, where people remain deaf to any deserving appeal from a person in distress and rarely lend them a helping hand.

Sitting in an army area, the contrast between people inside and outside couldn't have been starker for me, especially after listening to Deepak's story.

Most people outside the army compound are busy keeping pace with the fast moving world, all blindly accumulating material wealth. No one is free from its insidious influence.

But inside the compound, existed another world altogether. No one seemed to care about money. People selflessly served those in need, putting their own life and comfort at risk. Their only goal was to do the best for the nation. Happiness and pride lay in service rather than wealth.

But the world outside had forgotten that more possesions can never bring more happiness; rather, they bring more restlessness and discontentment. wealth obtained by mucky means only gives miseries.

The mind is always obsessing to protect his treasure. He gradually loses trust in everyone and becomes crippled physically and mentally. Soon old age approaches. All his dear companions depart from him one by one leaving him alone with him just wishing for final rest for his tired eyelids. The process of decline continues and soon his dear kids take over all his precious belongings and he drifts into oblivion.

Then, if he repents why he wasted time in accumulating so much wealth, it is too late.

We all know this, and yet the same race continues; and will continue.

I slipped deeper into my thoughts.

How many people are blessed with old age even? Isn't old age also a privilege, which many are denied like my dear husband who died without tasting its fruits?

So many times I would imagine how he would look at an advanced age? Whether he would have aged like me? Would he still be singing *bhajans* or what kind of life would he have led? How would Kashish have grown up? Whether he would have become a businessman or run a paint factory like his father? What would Parth have become? Would I have been a teacher or a housewife? So many similar questions plagued my mind.

Then I thought of Deepak's mother. We both must be around the same age and had faced similar tragedies. Does she also dream up these kinds of scenarios?

I felt small compared to Deepak's mother. She stood tall in comparison to me as she didn't let her morale wane even after seeing her husband die the death of a martyr. She still offered her sons to the nation.

Doesn't she worry for herself, I wondered?

I was thinking more about this, when Deepak returned with two pieces of good news.

Firstly, his brother had been located though not yet rescued. The army boat had gone to look for him as he lay trapped in another building in the cantonment area. Deepak was very happy on hearing his brother had been found.

The second piece of good news that made him happy was that his application had been accepted and he had finally been given permission to join the rescue mission.

Although I was shocked to hear this, a great sense of respect and gratitude arose in my heart for him.

It was 1 a.m.

We were getting extremely frustrated at the delay in the arrival of the plane. It became almost impossible to hang on to our patience any longer. People had started suggesting to the authorities, "Why don't you use one of these aircrafts parked here?"

One soldier explained that since the number of the passengers was quite large, those aircrafts wouldn't be of any use. In our case, a military transport aircraft or a cargo carrier would arrive so that all could be taken in one go.

We asked him what a cargo carrier was. He said that Military Transport Aircrafts are used to transport troops, ration, war equipment and weapons like guns, rifles, machine guns, cannons, rockets and, if needed, missiles too.

I was astonished at how a small looking airplane could carry rockets and missiles. He explained it in terms we could understand. He said they are like huge trucks that transport goods on ground. The cargo planes do that in the air. They carry supplies during wars or during calamities. They serve a number of purposes. For example, they were being used to drop passengers to Delhi at that time.

Deepak urged us to hold up for some more time as all such arrangements needed time and co-ordination.

Deepak's company and those determined army soldiers made me reconsider the definition of human beings.

On this earth, where people hardly do anything to help others, these warriors put their precious lives at stake to save strangers. And we just listen to their glorious victories, spend a moment to honour the sacrifice but pay no heed to the endless sufferings and woes they undergo.

So many of them never go back to meet their ailing old parents or wives or children. Emotions don't distract them from performing their duties.

Our nation buys garlands of triumphs at the cost of such valuable lives. But what do they get in return? Medals and trophies perhaps if they come back alive, unlike the cricketers and Olympians who are bestowed with enormous amounts of cash, lucrative gifts, immense recognition and popularity.

And if the warriors don't return from the battlefield, they get honourable tributes, which only their families get to see. They cannot enjoy the glory of their gallantry. Only in some special cases it happens that the government honors them by giving their worthy names to some roads or dispensaries but this again after many years of their deaths.

But what happens to the families afterwards? We forget that they have to undergo endless miseries for the rest of their lives. Nobody supports them and they have to continue on the journey of life alone just feeling pride at the sacrifice of a martyr.

But can only 'pride' provide bread. But maybe it hardly matters to them. They feel privileged to have spent a few years with their soldier souls.

Shouldn't it be the prime duty of our government to take care of their families after them?

Soon Deepak had to leave. He gave me his mobile number and asked me to call him if I needed any assistance.

He then left to carry on with the formalities and I kept on looking at him till the time he disappeared from my view. In only a few hours, he had left an impression on me that would never faint. We never come across such people in our routine lives in Delhi––so genuine, so good, so marvellous. I silently showered endless blessings on him!

But as soon as he disappeared from sight, my mind went back to my immediate concern. We were dying to meet our loved ones. I was anticipating that on seeing Kashish I would cry for many, many hours. Parth and I just wanted to be in his safe arms. We would cling to each other never to separate ever again. The feeling would be so divine!

My thoughts were interrupted by the announcement of the arrival of the aircraft.

That mighty aircraft, the passport to our freedom, finally arrived.

We were asked to form a queue. Without any hitch, everyone got up at once and completed the required formalities.

Once again, passengers' names were checked one by one and we were allowed to board the aircraft. Our eyes were full of tears and we hugged, thanked and blessed the army staff for saving our lives and sending us successfully to our destination.

I noticed that not only were we relived, the soldiers also displayed a sense of elation. After overcoming so many life-threatening hindrances, they had finally accomplished their goal. The spark of joy on the faces of the soldiers while helping us board the aircraft was unforgettable. It seemed as if they themselves were going to meet their loved ones.

Salute to their spirits!

The aircraft was exactly as Deepak had described to me. It was like an enormous closed truck without any luxuries. There were two big plain seats on which we were made to sit comfortably. The scene inside was scary though.

The sparse inside of that airplane left me surprised. Was this how soldiers are transported in times of war? They are stuffed in these bare aircrafts and dispatched to the battlefields.

In the normal course of life, we have only seen splendid aeroplanes with all facilities. Charming airhostesses flock to us fulfilling all our needs and making the entire journey enjoyable.

But this plane was devoid of even basic items like good seats to sit on. There were no frills at all. On the contrary, it was gloomy and lacked any warmth and comfort.

It pumped courage, inspiration and patriotism in our deflated spirits. We felt more respect and gratitude for our heroes.

It also made me think. Whenever these soldiers receive the call of duty, I'm sure it must be frightening for them too. When they enter these aircrafts, they might also feel scared like a normal person would. But they have to hide their fears and prepare themselves to answer stones from the opponents with bricks. How hard is it to enter the mouth of a canon willingly, that too without any self interest and just for the sake of the nation? This is simply too difficult for me to imagine.

All the people in the plane were sitting silently, relieved and filled with anticipation about meeting their families.

We all had seats. Unlike the comfortable seats of civil aircrafts, these were long, hard and uncomfortable benches. We clung to the others' bodies for balance and one by one fell into deep slumber. After so many upheavals, we finally found Goddess Nidra singing lullabies, making us fall into her lap.

The sound of the engine, though very harsh, provided us utmost peace.

I don't think I have ever had that kind of nap at any time in my whole life. Even if there is pin drop silence in my room in Delhi, I have to make an effort to catch a nap. But there, among many passengers, some of who were snoring, I enjoyed blissful slumber. No one was awake. We felt as safe with army men around us as a child feels with its parents.

We didn't know how much time it took but when I opened my eyes, we were informed that we had landed at Delhi's Army Airport. For a second, I felt my breath had stopped on hearing the word 'Delhi'.

Since last week, every moment we had been chanting the word––Delhi, Delhi and Delhi–– just as a saint chants his God's name. How would he feel if he is told that his Prophet has come in person to bless him? He would certainly lose his senses, at least for some seconds. We were in the same dazed condition.

We came out completely drained, with legs swollen and clothes covered in layers of mud. We were in the dirtiest clothes, our hair hard as rope, breath stinking, shoes torn and damp, and that small toothpaste still safe in my pocket. We had no sense of where to move.

We were walking like drunkards, hobbling and keeping each step with enormous effort.

Once again, we thanked the soldiers and blessed them with all our heart. Out of gratitude, we folded our hands as a mark of our thankfulness. We were crying and embracing complete strangers.

And finally, we stepped out onto the sacred land.

My soul, roaring loud
Was flying over the cloud.

Very calmly, patiently and sympathetically, the soldiers escorted us to the exit gate. At the airport gate, our names were checked in the list and we were allowed to go out.

It was 5:20 a.m.

It was dark and we were shivering in the chilly dawn. I don't know if it was the cold or our bodies had become accustomed to shivering. One by one, we came out after having suffered the worst days of our lives.

I came out crying uncontrollably and saw my son Kashish standing in front of me. He ran towards us and took me and Parth in his arms and loaded us with kisses and tears.

Those were exotic moments. I would have died in that moment happily, if God permitted.

No one spoke. We simply cried.

Many members of Anju and Neha's families were also present to greet them. None was in a condition to talk to the other. We just looked at them with teary eyes and got into our respective cars. We bade goodbye to each other and thanked God for extending our time on this planet.

Parth and I sat in the car with Kashish and Jayesh, his friend.

We didn't utter a single word; we only kept sobbing. His friend Jayesh tried to console us but in vain. It was not in our power to stop tears rolling down our cheeks.

Kashish tried to lighten the mood by saying, "Mummy, you have become very famous! You appeared on T.V. many times on news channels. Everybody saw you presenting your views."

I just nodded, still unable to speak.

Parth told him, "*Bhaiya*, they were interviews which were taken outside the helipad and at the Army Airport at Kashmir."

"The news of your being stranded in Kashmir is rife among all here. I suffered horrible pangs of separation and died each second. I made offerings to Gods, asked *mannats*[128], visited temples and gurudwaras and have been praying day and night for your safe return," Kashish continued.

He said that all his colleagues, friends and neighbours had been enquiring about us and putting up the same question about our safety and whereabouts day after day. Many acquaintances had seen Manoj and me on the news channels.

He kept on chattering but I couldn't utter a word. Rather, I was wondering whether the time had really come when I would be able to see my lavish bathroom again.

---

[128] *religious wish*

I was getting extremely impatient to shed my stinking clothes. I was dying to stand under the shower to feel the warm splash of soothing water on my real naked body.

Once I'm under the shower, I thought, I will not come out for hours.

It was insanely impossible for me to believe that I would be able to feel fresh water on my skin after so many days and bathe in so much clean water. My mind was caught up in that singular fantasy and I was hardly able to listen to what Kashish was babbling.

Water was the only thing I yearned for!

GLOSSARY

Chapter 1

kurta pyjama	*loose collarless long shirt and lose pants*
bhaijaan	*brother*
jijaji	*brother-in-law (sister's husband)*
masiha	*saviour*

Chapter 2

bhaiya	*Brother*
beta	*Son*
jawan	*Soldier*
maasi/ mausaji	*Aunt (Mother's sister)*
jaagran	*A religious wake where devotees stay awake all night singing devotional songs*
mamaji	*Uncle (Mother's brother)*
khandan	*clan*
Kuber	*Lord of wealth*
mandal	*a group of people who organize religious events for the community*
baniya	*A caste usually associated with business community*
bhajans	*devotional songs*

Maanga hai maine shyam se vardaan ek hi,	*I have asked for only one thing from Shyam,*
Teri kripa bani rahe jab tak hai zindagi.	*Shower your blessing on me all my life*
itr	*scent*
bhakti channels	*Devotional/God Channels*
Renu, mujhe Limca pilaa de, ye doctors tou mujhe maar hi daalenge.	*Renu, please get me some Limca. These doctors will kill me.*
beta, sab theek ho jayega.	*Child, all will be well*
pandits	*priests*
chachaji	*Uncle (father's brother)*

Chapter 3

dhokla	*A Gujrati delicacy*
poori	*Deep fried and puffed up bread*
karela subzi	*bittergourd curry*
namkeens	*salty snack*
shikara	*houseboat*
yuga	*mythological age (unit of time)*
di	*respectful epithet for elder sister*
bhakts	*devotees*

Chapter 5

boat aa gayi	*Boat has arrived*
JALDI CHALO! JALDI KARO!	*Hurry Up!*
Pagal ho gayi hai kya"? Ulti taraf kyo bhaag rahi hai	*Have you gone mad? Why are you running in the wrong direction?*

Chapter 6

bhutta	*roasted corn on cob*
kahwa	*Kashmiri tea*
nazakat	*elegance*
gol gappe	*street snack*
bhel puri	*street snack*
dhaba	*small roadside eatery*
bhaiya	*brother*

Chapter 7

chinar	*A deciduous tree*
airavata	*Mythological elephant belonging to Lord Indra, God of rain*
devas	*Gods*
yagna	*a fire ritual involving sacrifice*
rishi	*a sage*
tretayuga	*Second of the four ages in Hindu mythology*
rajma Chawal	*Rice and beans*
kari chawal	*Rice and chickpea flours and curd preparation*

Chapter 8

dosa	*rice and lentil savoury pancakes*
idli	*steamed cake of rice and lentil*
parantha	*stuffed flatbread, usually shallow fried*
miyan	*respectful epithet in urdu meaning sir, mister*

Chapter 9

jaldi aaoo, boat aa gayi hai	*Come fast! The boat has arrived*
mera beta! Usse bachaoo	*Save my son!*
namakpare	*Deep fried savoury snack*
mere bhai tune to meri jaan hi nikal di	*Dear brother! You nearly killed me!*

Chapter 10

Sirf tera hi aadmi fasaa hai? saare log hain wahan! Ja ek side mein beth ja!	*You think only your man is stuck? Go, sit in a corner!*
mere papa ko bachao uncle, please unhe bula do.	*Uncle, please save my Dad. Bring him back to me.*
khichdi	*a thick gruel of rice n lentils*
Dal	*lentils*

Chapter 11

toosh	*high-quality wool from the neck hair of the Himalayan ibex*
chapatis/roti	*flatbread*
pranayam	*breath exercise*
mehendi	*organic tattoo made of henna leaves*
churra	*a red and white bangle set newly wedded brides wear*
main hoon na	*I am here*
lungi	*cloth tied around waist extending to the ankles*

Chapter 12

Jaan	*darling*
ammi	*mother*

Chapter 13

yatra	*pilgrimage*
zindabad	*long live*
duppattas	*veil*
sarees	*saris*

Chapter 14

aloo sabzi	*potato curry*
amrit	*nectar*
henna	*a reddish-brown dye made from the powdered leaves of a tropical shrub, used to colour hair and decorate body*

| *Mumma ghar kab jayenge? Batao naa please* | *When will we go home Mom?* |

Chapter 15

| *mannat* | *religious wish* |

ACKNOWLEDGEMENTS

First and foremost, I thank Lord Govinda who let me be born in the pious family of Mr. and Mrs. Kashi Ram Aggarwal, my parents. They not only taught me the basic traits of a good human being but also taught me to have firm and undeterred faith in you.

My father, who despite modest finances, always encouraged me to get higher education and follow my ambition of being a writer. It is because of my parents' blessings that I have been able to conquer all odds and build a life I am very proud of.

I was not lucky enough to spend time in the sacred guardianship of my late father-in-law, Sh. Sneh Gupta, who died a few years before my marriage but have felt him showering blessings on us.

My late mother-in-law, Shri Premvati, always supported and guided me on how to rear kids with limited resources after my husband's demise.

I can't find words to express my gratitude to my brother-in-law Praveen who helped me when I fell short of finances in setting up a new venture. I am grateful to you for your generosity.

I am forever grateful to all my worthy teachers for their priceless education and inspirations.

My dear husband, Late Anil Mittal. I consider myself most fortunate to have tied the matrimonial knot with a man who was not only genuine but was deeply religious. He guided me on the path to spiritualism and to trust Shyam Baba unconditionally.

Though life with him was curtailed too soon, it was a miraculous one. He was my pillar of strength and I dedicate this book to him.

I also thank and whole heartedly bless my wonderful children, Kashish and Parth who faced the same tragedy that I did and always stood by me through thick and thin. Together we overcame all hurdles hand in hand, working hard to make a good life together.

My affectionate thanks to my brother Rajendra, sister-in-law Kusum and their sons Bhuvish and Parish for their sound counsel and encouragement in the most needed times.

My brother, very simple and kind hearted, understood the pangs of loneliness we were going through and never failed to come and comfort us on all festivals. He would sit for long hours with me and share my solitude and sadness. You were my true companion in those gloomy days. I love you my dear brother.

My heartfelt thanks to all my sisters:

Raj Rani and *jijaji* Late Sh.Raj Kumar
Meena, *Jijaji* Mr. Ramesh Aggarwal and her kids Mudit, Arpit and Garima
For the support and strength they provided me when we lacked it the most. They all did whatever best they could for us.
You all have treated us with utmost love and I reciprocate that sentiment.

My Ginni *Di* and *Jijaji* Mr. Ramesh Goel ..You and your kids Manit, Amit, Jyoti
Always cared my young Kashish and Parth in the years 2001-2004 which I can never forget. You considered my predicament as your own and have stood by us till today.
I could and still can bank upon this very family anytime for anything.
I don't have words to thank for all your favors, just endless blessings.

A very sincere thanks to my cousin brothers and sisters-in-law:

Dr. Anil, Aruna, Sumit and Anu. You always came to celebrate Diwali with us and shared our joys and sorrows.

I am greatly indebted to my respected in-laws for never letting me down and appreciating all my efforts:
Vijay *chachaji* and Sudha Chachiji who always encouraged me to move ahead in life despite all crisis. You and your sons Vivek, Arun and Neeraj always shared our tears and fears and contributed to your extents.

Subhash *chachaji* and Shakuntala Chachiji … you have always been there with us.

Late Sh.Chander *Mamaji*, Asha Mamiji and their sons Neeraj and Pankaj... your every little help meant a lot to us in those extreme days.

Mamaji, I have always missed your fatherly concern to all three of us.

My sisters-in-law:

Rashmi, Sunil *Jijaji* and their kids Gaurang and Tanvi Sangeeta and Ashok *Jijaji*
You were there when all had left and I am hardly able to thank your for your help.

My special thanks to the committee members of the CA Apartments, who understood my trauma and time. They never forced me to clear the dues and gave me ample of time.

My gratitudes to my neighbours Reema chawla and her father, Kiran Seth, Heena Bhatia and other Acquaintances of C.A. Apts. Kiran Wadhwa, Mr. Sanjay Shashtri (Pandit Ji), Mr. and Mrs. Radhey Mohan Aggarwal ..I will be forever grateful to all of you for your moral support and comforting words during our crisis.

Mr. S.P. Taneja (yoga instructor) who always encouraged me to join yoga classes to stay stress free. Thank you uncle for your care and compassion.

I would also like to thank:

Viresh Dabbas, Devendra Umrao, N.M.Sudhir, Ajay Suri, Ashu Punjabi (the singer), Girish Johar and many others for helping in managing so many successful events during my Event Management years.

Special thanks to:

Dear Sweety, Hardeep, Mr. Pramod and Rita Jain, all my students and their parents...Thank you so much for vesting trust in my teaching ability at the time I was just starting out.

My deeply heartfelt thanks to
Mr. Dilip Ghosh (Former Joint Director, News, All India Radio), who showed me the right way to write this book... Dada I can't thank you enough for all your guidance and assistance.

At length my sincere most thanks to

Our honorable Prime Minister Mr Narendra Modi

Every single soldier, *jawan* and officer of.... JK Police, our Indian Army, Indian Navy and Indian Air Force
All the staff members of CH2 Hotel
And all the local Kashmiris and our Muslim brothers...

It was the result of the solidarity and the resolute and chivalric efforts of all of you that helped to accomplish the unaccomplishable task of saving lakhs of people from the claws of death.

The gratitude to you is beyond words
Just Salute to the Saviors!
... May Almighty shower his choicest blessings on all of you!